D1443773

Above and Below Ground

Marilyn Massey

'Hard Sauce'

HARD SAUCE, the author's personal dog. A winner in conformation classes he is a tough, courageous worker "Above & Below Ground," always a gentleman and a perfect travelling companion. To date he has sired over 125 puppies.

Above and Below Ground

The Jack Russell Terrier
in
North America

**Stories, Photographs, Selection,
Training and History**

by
Marilyn Massey

A Book for all Dog Lovers

©1985
Woodluck Publications, Millwood, Virginia

To Alex

My adored husband, whose support and love for me, plus his doubts that I would finish this book, kept me writing and photographing.

Table of Contents

Short Sentences from letters written to the author and to Ailsa
Crawford about their Jack Russell Terriers—throughout the
book.

"JIG is a most beloved companion and has the most enthusiastic outlook on life of any animal I have ever encountered.

She is very well behaved and extremely sensitive to verbal punishment. This trait has allowed her to be easily trained and disciplined."

Preface

To have met him was to love him—his crooked nose, his crazy ears, his short misshapen legs and his glorious contagious smile— was he a Jack Russell Terrier? Not by a long shot; but he WAS a terrier and he was white and brown, with a hard rough coat—a little guy, ready to take on the world. It was his courage that was his undoing. A few days before his fourth birthday he took on three large dogs, protecting his female love. Maxted was to start a very special endeavour. We had no way of knowing, when we bought that first irresistible terrier for our daughter Caroline, we had been hooked for life. When Maxted was killed, 12 year old Caroline was recuperating from a serious illness (mononucleosis and hepatitis). Everyone felt it would be good therapy for her, to replace him as soon as possible. So, we made a trans-Atlantic phone call to Bert Pateman, kennel huntsman to the Duke of Beaufort, who, accord- ing to our researches, was one of the best terrier breeders in England. We closed a deal on a 10 month old, white, rough coated bitch: "One of the best I've ever bred." We then made another call to England, this time to our dear friend Kay (Mrs. Babe) Moseley, who lived close to Badminton. She generously agreed to take the puppy up to London and send her by plane to Caroline. Days went by and finally one morning this cable was phoned to us, addressed simply "Caroline" with an accompanying phone number!

"Arriving Washington 6:30 p.m. Stop. Hope you will love me."

No sender's name. No mention of which airline she was on—panic! We knew it was information about the terrier's arrival and that somehow the cable had arrived incomplete. After several phone calls we narrowed it down to a Pan Am flight which was scheduled to arrive at Dulles International at 6:30 p.m. Our sleuthing had been correct—and there, amongst three hundred monkeys was a crate with a tag on it addressed to Caroline.

We had expected something like the little character Maxted or the small, bull-dog type white terriers we had seen around—so when a lovely, beautifully balanced, 14 inch rough coated dog, with "black raisins for eyes and a currant for a nose," bounded out of the kennel showing no signs of fright, insecurity or flight fatigue, we were quite taken aback. A second look and we realized that Bert Pateman had sent us a star! I am sure that Parson Russell would have approved this bitch as a founder of a dynasty of good hunting terriers in Virginia. Her conformation read like the breed standard. She was beaten only once in conformation classes, held at Hound Shows (these terrier classes were in their infancy 20 years ago) under several different English judges—Caroline named her Tempest.

Shortly after Tempest's arrival, we acquired a rough coated male dog, the produce of imported English stock, for our daughter Denya. Although his conformation wasn't perfect, he had a marvelous head and straight front legs, but above all he had a super disposition—more good luck! So these two embarked us on a breeding programme we hadn't planned! Ten generations later the good disposition, working ability and splendid conformation of these two terriers continues to stamp our terriers today.

It is interesting that the conformation of top terriers in North America and England look so much like the terriers in nineteenth century paintings by Emms, J. M. Tracey, Osthaus, Ferneley, etc. It appears that the type of terrier which conforms to the Jack Russell Terrier breed standard in both the British Isles and North America is like Parson Jack Russell's terriers judging from available photographs of his dogs and their descriptions found in various books and articles.

Introduction

From the beginning, the "Jack Russell" terrier has been bred for brains, hunting ability, independence and companionship. His ancestors go back to the start of the nineteenth century. We have paintings showing white terriers from that era, which to-day would pass as Jack Russell Terriers. His versatility makes him a suitable pet for most situations, where some outdoor activity takes place. He is not suitable as an apartment dog—where he is walked on a leash as his only exercise. Hunting and running are his love. A rubber ball thrown as far as it can be thrown, never loses it's thrill—the chase, the efforts to kill it and the expectancy of another throw! He is, of course, by nature a "go-to-ground" dog (terra meaning earth or ground). He has been bred to go into a hole and "mark" the game (by barking, scratching, etc.). Although he is not expected to kill the hunted game, he must be strong and feisty enough to protect himself against ferocious animals such as the badger, cornered raccoon, groundhog, etc. and to be able to kill them only if necessary.

Why is he so popular as a pet? It is because he is really a schizophrenic! In the house he is a love, a charmer, an entertainer with a marvelous sense of humour, a co-operative member of the household, a babysitter, and a sick-bed comforter and consoler.

3

He often is low key, giving you to know for certain that he has no interest in snarling foxes, biting groundhogs, vicious otter and mink or balled-up, terrifying raccoons. If he is properly brought up, he is beautifully behaved—full of personality and character.

But outside when he is hunting he can become another animal you wouldn't dare let darling two year old Susie anywhere near! He is not only courageous beyond his ability, but he is deliriously happy the minute he senses game afoot. His tenacity, gameness and willingness to return to the attack will continue until he is stopped by his handler or until he or his adversary drop from exhaustion or kill. In this, he shows no discretion, and it is up to his owner to know when to call a halt, and not selfishly let him continue, just because he (the owner) is getting such a charge out of it, at his poor dog's expense. It must be remembered at all times the terrier's first job in life is to MARK, and not to kill the quarry. When he is below ground, for him to try to kill a fox, badger, raccoon, etc. is practically suicidal. His job is to make enough noise and/or racket so the digger above will know where to dig in order to let the quarry out—to be hunted again by waiting hounds.

Throughout the book the pronoun for the Terrier will be "he." I am not ignoring the E.R.A., but it makes better reading to say "he" rather than "he/she." I have no preference between a bitch and a dog. When it is necessary to use a name, I have chosen to call our hero "Static."

The "one line statements" spaced throughout the book, are quotes from letters written by owners of Jack Russell Terriers to Mrs. Ailsa Crawford and to the author about their terriers. They are included because they give great insight into the character, personality and popularity of the Jack Russell Terrier.

Although I have tried to keep this book strictly about terriers in North America, I have included reproductions of nineteenth century British oil paintings and two articles by British authors. In all cases they are to help the reader understand not only the background of the Jack Russell but that the modern breed standard is a concentrated effort to reproduce the type of hunt terrier that was used for going-to-ground, as early as 1820, not only by Parson Jack Russell, but by other enthusiastic fox-hunters.

There have been many British books written on the Jack Russell Terrier, but this is the first one to be devoted to the Jack Russell Terrier in North America. The chapters are short, informative and hopefully, helpful. The personality, conformation, companionship, intelligence, versatility and working ability of Jack Russell Terriers will be brought out through pictures, anecdotes and short statements from owners.

Please, lets call this marvelous dog by his *proper* name—a Jack Russell. He is *not* a Jack, that is a male donkey or mule. He is *not* a Russell, that is the surname of thousands of people. And please, not "J.R."—Isn't he a notorious oil wheeler dealer that only his mother loves?

THE SCHIZOPHRENIC

In the house he is a love, a charmer . . .

But outside he can become quite another animal . . .

"RIBBONS AND POINTS" owned by Mrs. Ralph Miller, and bred by Mrs. George Kandra, Maryland.

After a day of showing in Pennsylvania, a group of breeders took their terriers for a swim in the creek that ran through the show grounds. In this photo, there are eleven dogs (two of them belonging to the judge). Most of them are champions. They chased a stick and splashed around together with no signs of fighting. An unforgettable ending to a hot day!

Acknowledgements

This book never could have reached fruition without the help and encouragement of so many people—some of them terrier owners, but many just good friends with skills unknown to me. First is first—so I acknowledge the terriers who have made our busy, diversified and happy life more interesting, more joyous and even more diversified. Their companionship, love of sport, unquestioning devotion and their continually thinking up something new, is a facet in my life that I would not change in any way. They have affected our whole family, permanently.

Who next? It is Frank Scheder, owner and manager of the local photography store in Winchester, Virginia. He, because he started me on my career (if it can be called that) of photography. He, himself a brilliant technician, literally had to teach me how to develop film and print pictures—and I mean, he had to start from scratch. In 1966, when I started—I hadn't a clue what I was supposed to do! With never ending patience he answered all my silly questions. He steered me back on the right course when I went off on a tangent, encouraged me, sold me only what I needed and showed me all the short cuts. There were times when he just plain told me exactly what to do. I can recall, when running into some difficulty half way through developing a film or making a print, phoning him directly from my dark room and he would solve the problem immediately! And so, with him as my mentor I produced the photographs in this book which is what started my idea of an American Jack Russell Terrier Book—thank you Frank, I owe you so much.

I want to thank my housekeeper, Sandy Rosenberger, who always was there to make my days easier. So often she held puppies and dogs for photographs, often in quite unusual situations—she's known as the stage manager of Woodluck Kennels! She cheerfully ran messages, stuffed advance notices in envelopes, picked up and delivered things and generally did many jobs not pertaining to her work, so I would have more time for the book.

Anyone who has read the acknowledgements in my husband's last three books knows the name Peggy Williams. If there is a faster, more accurte, more agreeable typist, I have yet to meet her. On dull days, her pleasant voice saying "that's no problem, I can do that for you" made things seem so simple. There were times she must have despaired when she found the same piece of writing back for a third typing. If she did, she never let me know. Beth Carnes, who herself is a book promoter and is responsible for the promotion and distribution of this book, kept my enthusiasm going with her continual "It's wonderful—I wish it were beside my bed right now." Then there are all the super people who took the time and effort to send me contributions—without them the first half of the book (short stories) could not have been written.

When I first phoned Ailsa Crawford, President of the J.R.T.C.A. and told her what I was up to, I was not prepared for her spontaneous endorsement and encouragement. This provided a great "spurt of energy" on my part. Paul Ross, the Lowerys and Wingate Mackay-Smith's excellent contributions to the book are so much appreciated. Paul, on his favorite subject, History of the Jack Russell, was so kind to condense his extensive history knowledge into one chapter—I know he could write a book on the subject. The Lowerys were marvelous for attacking the subject of "Working Your Terriers," for me. They write from personal, up-front experience and I feel very lucky to have this chapter. Wingate Mackay-Smith is one of, if not the top breeder, show kennel and international judge of Bull Terriers in the world (don't worry, she has bred and raised many Jack Russells). Her amusing chapter on Training and Showing Your Terrier is guaranteed to produce a chuckle—

but is also very, very good and a help to anyone who wants to show their terriers in conformation classes.

The delightful, humorous drawings by Pamela Edwards, Quebec Canada, really add a marvelous touch to the book. I was so lucky to "catch her" when she was visiting a friend, a few miles from me. Her enthusiasm for my writing and her willingness to work quickly produced these pin and ink drawings in a few days! Rita King's super drawings, which appear at the head of the chapters, certainly make the book more appealing.

At the risk of leaving out a name, I now just want to thank all of you who encouraged, wrote, phoned and did so many things to keep me going!

I especially want to acknowledge the support and continual help my youngest daughter Caroline has given me. Many times, when on the verge of doing something else, she would cheerfully change her plans and lend me a hand. She spent over three hours, each day, looking after the dogs, puppies, kennels, etc., so that I would have the time to work on my book, free of that responsibility. She never let me waver and always laughed at my doubts or worries.

Last but best, is my wonderful husband, Alex, who read my manuscript, edited it, corrected my spelling etc. and often made excellent suggestions to improve the text. Most importantly, he would raise my spirits when, after plowing through one of my badly handwritten chapters, he would look over his glasses at me, and say "that's great, Mum." With all the writing HE was doing, to take the time from his work, to do this for me, was surely a gift of love.

Short Stories

A Tribute

If you have owned the one who never deserted you,
Who in this selfish world was your unselfish friend,
Who never proved ungrateful, mean or treacherous,
Who gave his steadfast trust, and tried to comprehend.
Whose sensitivity sought out your every mood,
Who gave so much and asked from you so little,
Who, when all the world was doubting and unsure,
remained supportive, loyal and undoubting—
Then sure it was a Jack Russell, who blessed you for a friend.

Marilyn Mackay-Smith
from thoughts of Sharon Floro—1981

"Maybe it's an owner's prejudice, but I think he's beautiful. He's a super little dog. By the time he was six months old he had killed four rats. He was very low key about it all, and goes about hunting in a very matter of fact way. The first rat he killed, came down from a feed chute and as it dropped he caught it in mid air. It was dead before it hit the ground! He just dropped it, and wandered off like it was very unimportant."

Annie Takes a Ride

I own two Jack Russell Terriers. Maggie is two and a half years old, and her daughter, Annie, is six months old. Both dogs, especially the puppy Annie, love to play with my barn cat, Motor. Annie jumps on Motor's back, grabs her by the scruff of her neck, and they roll around on the ground like a couple of playful bear cubs! They then take turns chasing each other.

Every night, we make a trip to the barn to feed the horses. Annie and Maggie look forward to this, because they know they will get a handful of pellets. One night, instead of their usual "race to the barn" they went in the other direction. A few seconds later, Annie came around the corner, riding on the back of what we, at first, thought was Motor. We were pretty amused until we realized that Motor does not have a white strip down her back! The skunk was spraying all over, as Annie hung on, while Maggie and I watched. The skunk ran past us, and took off into the bushes, with Annie still on its back!! Maggie and I fed the horses, and finally Annie came running in for her share of the pellets. The whole area smelled of skunk. It wasn't until we got back to the house, I realized neither dog had been sprayed (or bitten)!

—Arlette Johnson

annie came around the corner, riding what we thought was Motor.

Rescue at Sea

Maine is a wonderful place to visit in the summer, especially when the temperatures at home go into the nineties, so we felt very lucky when, along with our Jack Russell Terrier, Kipper we were invited for a week's stay on the Island in the Penobscot, known as Dark Harbor or Isleboro. Typically, Kipper is always interested in doing whatever the family does, and often he finds himself in very strange situations (for a dog, that is). Boats are not usually part of a terrier's life, but Kipper soon developed sea legs and became quite cocky on board, running along the gunnel, even out onto the bowsprit, barking at the wake, as we slipped through the water, holding his head high, sniffing the breezes. All went well and he soon had added to his name "Seaman First Class!"

A few days passed, uneventfully, but then, one day, "Seaman First Class" degraded himself while sailing in a stiff breeze in the Penobscot Bay, when he became a bit too cocky and fell overboard! The Maine water is not exactly warm, as most know from bitter experience, and the small sloop in which we were sailing had no motor power to use for a quick turn around. Now what!! As I was at the tiller, daughter Jane was tending the sails, so it was up to poor Den, my husband to make the rescue. (He had announced earlier in the day, when I mentioned that Kipper should be put below, that he would jump in after him, if he fell overboard, never thinking that it would really happen.) So, yes indeed, over Den went, clothes, shoes, watch and all, to the rescue of "The Seaman." The shock of hitting the cold water, knocked the wind from him for a brief moment, but he soon recovered, when he saw that Kipper, only a few feet away, was loosing ground and starting to sink. He swam like crazy, reached the dog and held him up. By this time, I had been able to "come about" and throw a life cushion to them. Kipper was the first to catch it, as, of course, Den's hands were busy holding Kipper. Kipper held onto the cushion, giving both Den and himself a certain amount of buoyancy. I came about again, luffed all sails, stopping, to a certain extent, all forward motion, and grabbed, with the help of Jane, both boys, pulling them aboard. By this time, Kipper's gums were sheet white from shock and freezing cold and Den was not much better. Thank goodness we were not far from our dock, and hurried home as fast as we could. Once home, a good fast rub for Kipper soon brought color back to his mouth. A hot shower and drink for my husband, put Kipper back in good standing. The experience, one would think, would put off a dog from going around water or boats again—oh no, not a Jack Russell—would you believe, the next morning Kipper could hardly wait to get back on board!

—Ailsa Crawford

and soon he added to his name "Seaman First Class."

What's Holding Up Dinner?

My Jack Russell Terrier puppies, Woodluck Saffron and Woodluck Tornado, are a constant thrill to me. When they were eight months old, both the bitch and the dog put a fox in an earth and proceeded taking turns "going to ground." Unfortunately, there was no exit, so he could not be bolted. The pups both dug with boundless energy, until they reached their quarry. Quite suddenly, they realized they were not sure what they should do next, so they retreated to ask "Mom" about the matter. Meanwhile "Mom" was having cardiac arrest, convinced the raging red beast was going to murder her babies. I was no help at all at first. Just as I got my mind on the task at hand, Old Red bolted from the earth. The chase was on! The pups ran like troupers, giving tongue all the way. The fox made a nice circle and came back past where I was standing, with the two Jack Russell puppies in hot pursuit. After making a second circle, he came near me again and I was able to get the puppies off the line, and rewarded them with several pats. At this point, it was almost 8:00 p.m. and I was a mile from home. By the time we arrived home, my family was not sure what to think. I suppose not many Moms walk in at such an hour, grinning from ear to ear, clutching two dirty, hot, wet Jack Russell Terrier puppies.

—Marsha Corum

The Jack Russell as a Mother Sheep

My Jack Russell bitch, Penny, used to be my number one assistant at lambing time. I would bring chilled or neglected newborns into the house and put them by the woodstove in the kitchen. Penny would then take over, licking them dry and pushing them around with her nose to get them on their feet. While she was doing this, I would go back to the barn to get some milk from the mother ewe for her lamb. After being warmed, dried, and fed the ewe's milk, the lamb would be ready to return to the barn and its mother. Penny helped me save many lambs this way.

–Lynne Westaway.

Kipper Finds a New Occupation

Every day, rain or shine, Kipper comes up to the stable, to join us on the morning drives, be it with a single pony, pair, tandem, unicorn or four-in-hand. When the vehicle I am using is rolled out of the carriage house, he takes up his position under the axle and sits waiting for the ponies to be put to. Sometimes, if it seems to take too long, he will rush over to me, give a few little barks, as if to say, "Let's go," and then rushes back to his position, lest another terrier take his place, or we should move off without him. Finally, I give the ponies the command to move off, and down the road we go, with Kipper under the axle. No matter where I go, or what I do, Kipper will stay there until we are back at the stable again, and the drive has finished. Many times, when I am asked to put on a driving exhibition away from home, I am also requested to bring along Kipper. He seems to have become part of the show. Being basically white in color, he goes quite well with my white Welsh ponies, who seem to enjoy his company. So it seems, that this gay little breed of terriers enjoys the job once done by the Dalmatian. His fondness to run and take exercise has made it possible for him to become a necessary adjunct of my driving turnout. And so it is, the Jack Russell Terrier joins the sport of coaching, and adds his presence to yet another field in the world of sport.

—Ailsa Crawford

It's Mine!

On our trip west, we had been told about a place where we could dig for petrified wood. So off we went, armed with pick and shovel. As we never went anywhere without our Jack Russell Terrier bitch, Bronwyn, she came along to help us look. She had a great time running back and forth between us. Across the road, on a hillside, were a man and woman digging. We decided to cross over and speak to them. It turned out they had a rock shop and were digging for large pieces of petrified wood. The woman had a geology pick and had loosened some dirt, which caused Bronwyn to dig madly. After sending mother earth in all directions, she dug out a sizeable piece of quartzite! She tried to pick it up, but it was too large and heavy for her mouth. Then the woman tried to pick it up, but soon let go of it, when Bronwyn went Grrrrrr. It was HER rock. Fortunately for all of us, the woman thought she was darling and was greatly amused by her behavior. My husband put the rock in his pail and Bronwyn danced around on her hind legs trying to get it. We were allowed to keep it and brought it back with us. Do you know Bronwyn still plays with it at home! She can't pick it up, so she pushes it around with her nose, all over the house. She knows, after all it is still HERS!

—Jill Affelbaum

Rats in the Belfry

We were eagerly looking forward to a four day equestrian clinic in Tallahassee, Florida—not only for the chance to improve our riding and our horses, but because it gave us a four day sabatical away from our busy schedule at the farm and our tack shop business. Besides bringing our two horses, we brought our two Jack Russell Terriers, Woodluck-South Bean Sprout who was one year old, and By Golly, who was seven months old. We take the "kids" everywhere with us. As we had owned By Golly for just a couple of months she had gone to only two shows with us, since there aren't any shows during the summer in Florida. On the other hand, Bean was a seasoned traveler, having taken in the winter circuit. He is well known and takes everything in stride, with a calm and cool attitude, and with an air that says he knows he is something special. He has joined me on three winning victory gallops by sitting, in front of my saddle, on my horse. Both terriers are very well behaved when we travel, but By Golly has to wear a leather collar with a bell because she has such keen hunting instincts that, once she is on a scent, she is oblivious to any sound, let along coming when called!

We arrived at our destination just before dark. The next day was a busy one. We had the two horses to ride, as well as doing news spots and interviews with both the newspaper and a television crew. At first we put By Golly and Bean on leashes because there were so many smells and animals to check out. After a while, as Bean has seniority over By Golly and a sharper ear for our commands, we let him loose. Somehow, my husband got elected to be interpreter between a man who had a knowledge of the art and intricacies of dressage, and a person from the paper who hardly knew the difference between trot and canter, let alone passage and piaffe! By this time, J. C. (my husband) had let By Golly off her leash, but was keeping an eye on the two dogs, as he talked to the reporter and the instructor.

Sometime during this technical conversation, the "kids" slipped away on a hunting venture. When we realized they were gone, we started a search that took in every nook and cranny of the farm. We finally found Bean Sprout at an old slave church, dating back to the early nineteenth century, which had been moved to the farm a few years ago by one of the past owners. The building measures about 30 feet from the ground to the edge of the roof. At this point the roof goes up a steep 45° angle. There is a bell tower on the front. The back of the church is attached to the indoor riding school, forming a gallery or stage for it. Inside the church there is no way to climb into the bell tower. The inside ceiling of the church goes up at an angle and then levels off to a flat ceiling higher up. Bean Sprout, although he was doing some hunting under the church, was spending most of the time looking up the walls. We thought By Golly might be in there—but even with the help of a flashlight we couldn't see or hear any sign of her. We enlisted Bean Sprout's help in finding her and together we walked all through the surrounding fields and woods. We drove around the neighboring farms and houses, asking everyone we saw if they had seen a little white dog with a black eye and ear, and to call us if they found her. We also enlisted the children in the area to look for her when they were riding their bikes. We were worried she was lost, being in a strange place, or that someone had picked her up, seeing how cute and friendly she was. She was nowhere to be found. We searched on horseback, and from the truck. When night came we finally resigned ourselves to giving up until daylight. We attended the clinic dinner party and watched ourselves riding on television, and listened to the interviews with the newsman; but the fun of the evening was clouded by the fact there would be no By Golly in the camper when we went back that night. How were we ever going to tell Marilyn Mackay-Smith we had lost her? Both Bean Sprout and By Golly were by her champion dog, Hard Sauce, and By Golly was out of the bitch Dolly, who was Grand Champion two years in a row at the Virginia Foxhound Show. We had wheedled and cajoled these two pups from her which she had planned to keep for herself. They were to be our foundation stock for our Jack Russell Terrier Kennels. We had promised a bitch pup back to her, out of By Golly's first litter. Would there be a first litter now? Once more we called and listened for the tinkle of By Golly's bell, but no luck.

The next morning, at the crack of dawn, my first thought was that it had been a bad dream, but J. C. shattered that, by saying he was going to take the truck and Bean Sprout to see if he could find By Golly. I decided I'd keep myself busy by feeding my horses.

While mixing the feed, I heard an eerie howl. OH OWWOEE! It seemed to be coming from the direction of the church! My heart skipped a beat. The long howl stopped. I wasn't sure whether the church was haunted or maybe, just maybe, it was By Golly. I called her name and ran towards the church, hoping the howl would start again, enabling me to pinpoint it. The only problem was that she never barks when you call her. OH OWWOEE. I was closer now. It sounded as though it had come from high up in the church. I ran inside and looked up at the ceiling and started calling her. No answer. I stopped and listened for a moment. TINKLE, TINKLE, TINKLE. It was her! She was on the floor of the bell tower, 30 feet above me!

I ran to get some help (J. C. was out in the truck, searching for her, with Bean Sprout). I found a long aluminum construction ladder, and put it up against the inside wall. When I made it to the very top of the ladder, I finally saw her! However, she refused to come down the angled ceiling that ran up the sides of the building to the belfry floor. Fortunately some of the floor boards were dry rotted, so by using all my strength to break them, I could shove my hand in through the boards where I could just barely touch her. As the tower was totally closed in, I had to make a small hole, through which I would be able to pull her out. Somehow I got hold of her front leg, and pulled her through the opening, into my arms. She was very glad to see me, but nervous about our being up so high on top of a ladder. Little did she know I was petrified! We went down the ladder very slowly. She couldn't have been any happier than I was when we reached the bottom. What a joyful reunion the four of us had when J. C. and Bean Sprout finally came back from their empty search.

There remained one puzzling thing. How in the world did she climb all the way up into the ceiling of the church? We went back to the church to try to figure it out. As there were no stairs we knew she couldn't have gone up from the inside. When we inspected underneath we discovered that, between the exterior wall and the interior wall of the church which were both made of boards lying horizontally, there was a space of about eight inches between the two walls. Concrete pillars, about three feet off the ground, supported the walls. Now it made sense when Bean Sprout kept standing underneath looking up towards the floor. They must have been hunting rats and By Golly, in the excitement of the hunt, shinnied up the space between the walls, by pushing her paws on one wall and her back and neck against the other wall. Arriving at the top, still determined to get that varmint, she went up the angled ceiling to the floor of the belfry. Knowing By Golly, she probably got the rat! The fun over, she didn't know how to get down.

You might think this was the end. But no. Three weeks later, we went back to the same farm for another clinic—you guessed it—in no time, By Golly was missing and yes, she was in the belfry again! At least, this time we knew how to get her down.

—Leslie Smith

TRIPLE HAPPY. Bred by Gary Biemiller and presently owned by Mr. and Mrs. Robert Gogarty. His roots are Virginian, having a great deal of Heritage Kennel breeding in his pedigree, and going back to Ray Pearson's Minor, who was an unbeatable terrier in his day. (see page 172)

"She is the greatest dog. She has really proved her stuff. We all love her so."

Who's Got the Car Keys?

If you've been lucky enough to own one Jack Russell Terrier at a time, with no children to bring up, or chickens to feed, or horses to "muck-out", etc., you will know that very soon he becomes almost human, and it is just about impossible to get a "one upmanship" on him and outsmart him. Woodluck Teflon is just such a dog. He came to us from Virginia, when he was a seven week old puppy. My husband is retired, our son has been on his own for a long time, so he soon became our dearest child and companion, one who has a mind as sharp as his intelligent head leads you to believe!

Like most Jack Russell Terriers, next to hunting, car-riding is his great love—and any suggestion of one in the offing, sends him into a frenzy of joy! One day, I was getting ready to go out, but hadn't put on my coat when Tefie trotted into the kitchen and dropped my *car keys* on the floor. He kept picking them up and dropping them, trying to get my attention. I finally looked to see what on earth he was doing. Obviously, he wanted me to hurry up and get in the car! I was astounded at his apparent reasoning—but thought it was probably a coincidence. Not so, this was repeated several days in a row. I then decided discretion was a better course to follow, so instead of leaving the keys on the hall table as usual, I left them in my purse. I suppose I shouldn't have been surprised, but, when the next day I was presented with my purse, I was amazed! I then took to hiding the keys—that was also useless, as he always found them and brought them to me! The crowning glory, however, was the time that neither Tefie nor I could find the keys in spite of searching everywhere. I was sitting rather desolately on the couch, wondering what to do—when I felt Tefie nudge me—I looked down and Bless Pat, if he hadn't found a long lost set of keys, we had given up ever seeing again. (They belonged to my mother's car, but Tefie knew they were car keys, and that was what mattered to him.)

—Mr. & Mrs. Robert Smith

Teamwork

Tempest (a white, rough coated bitch, from the Duke of Beaufort's Hunt, England) had been in this country, as a new member of our family, for only a few days, when I was allowed to take her riding with me and the Bouvier des Flandres (Dinwiddie). I was warned to keep an eye on her and not to let her get into any trouble. Quite a responsibility! Everything was going wonderfully—one squirrel treed, one groundhog put to ground, and several rabbits left with rapidly beating hearts in various brush piles, when to my horror, I noticed Tempest dragging one of her hind legs—obviously in great distress. I was about to jump off my horse when I noticed the Bouvier intently watching something. I followed his stare and saw a bull groundhog slowly following Tempest, with apparent curiosity. For once, I sat still and did nothing. Tempest continued her laborious way, as did Mr. Groundhog. All of a sudden, the scene changed—with a great rush and a leap, Dinwiddie had the varmit and, with a mighty SNAP, broke his back and it was all over. Tempest, who was of course, absolutely fine, gave it a few good shakes to show that she was part of the show.

How did she know, not a native of this country and only in residence a few days, to play this "broken wing" trick? She and Dinwiddie, and later other terriers, teamed up, time after time, to work out some arrangement where they would draw the quarry away from his hole and then Dinwiddie would deal the final blow!

—D.T.

Jack Tries to Save Judy

Jack and Judy were outside one very cold winter day and I was working by the window when I saw Jack who was out in the field, race to the back door, throw himself at it and take off again back to the field. As Judy, who was always with him, was nowhere to be seen, I wondered if she might be in trouble. I left the window and heard Jack hit the back door twice more, while I was frantically putting on my coat and boots. I ran after Jack, who again was heading back toward the field. The only thing I could think of that could possibly be considered dangerous, was a small stream, now mostly frozen over, and it was in this direction that Jack was heading. I became afraid that Judy might have fallen in somehow, and I began calling her name to let her know I was coming, hoping if she was in the water it would keep her from giving up. All of a sudden Jack stopped, and then, just casually wandered off. I continued on and, as I feared, there was the evidence that Judy had fallen into the stream at its only really deep spot. Her claw marks where she had struggled to get out were all around the frozen snow at the banks. I don't know how Jack knew enough to come to the house for help, nor do I know how he knew the exact moment that we were too late.

—Lynne Westaway

TEMPEST, the author's first Jack Russell Terrier owned by her daughter Caroline Treviranus.
painting by Pamela Edwards, 1973.

These two terriers, owned by William Bermingham, M.F.H., President of the Master of Fox Hounds Association (of America) and Master of the Hamilton Hunt, Ontario, Canada entertained the crowd at the 1985 Canadian Fox Hound Show, London, Ontario, by running this soccer ball around the show ring. They have complete control over it, and would bring it back to their owner on command!

Nothing warmer than Hudson's Bay mittens.

A model of a beautiful, correct head.

WOODLUCK ÉCLAIR, owned by José Rico, a frequent winner in conformation classes.

A level group of puppies from two different, but closely related, litters.

Where's My Driver?

Slurpy's big day had arrived! His chance to prove his manhood was imminent as Tempest was waiting for him at the local kennels, having spent fourteen days there, in anticipation of his visit. Our farm manager got the nod to use the farm station wagon to take Slurpy to meet his love. Off they went and everything happened, just as it was supposed to! The usual two days later, Slurpy made the same trip in the station wagon, and again, all went well. Apparently, Slurpy had got the message—because the next morning, when the farm manager came to work, there was Slurpy, sitting on the back seat of the station wagon!

—Denya

Ben Tries Flying

Our new stable was finally completed, but Wilbur, the stable cat refused to accept it as his new home. It was only after he had jogged back to the old stable many times, to be returned to the new one, that he was finally persuaded to move permanently. Unlike the old loft, that had a ladder, the new stable has stairs, which allows for a much better cat chase by our terriers (Wilbur having dodged them many times, by a rapid climb up the ladder!). One day, when my husband and I were in the tack room, we heard a loud thump, followed by whines. Upon investigation, we discovered that Ben, our male Jack Russell Terrier, apparently had been in hot pursuit behind Wilbur, when Wilbur decided he had had enough, and jumped down through one of the hay drops, into the stall below. Ben followed suit, and 12 feet later, had only his injured pride to show for his efforts!! No harm done, but from then on the cat chases were held to ground level!!

—Mrs. C. Martin Wood III

"He is the most handsome little guy with a fantastic personality. He has really dented the muskrat population around here not to mention the squirrels—I am amazed at his hunting ability at so young an age."

"Deer" Duchess

My Jack Russell Terrier bitch, Duchess, was a little over a year old, and she still had not seen a deer, dead or alive. So, when my foreman had killed a large buck, and brought it back to the farm, to be hung and dressed, I thought it advisable to leave her in the house because she might be frightened of it—Right now, you can tell this was my first Jack Russell Terrier! Somehow, she slipped out of the house and made straight for the buck, who was still in the truck, with his head hanging over the tailgate. She jumped in the air grabbed his nose and hung on! We waited for her to drop to the cement—but nothing doing. We called, cajolled, ordered—and still she hung on. We had a hoist for hanging deer, off the ground, so we could dress them. The buck was already to go up "Pull him on up" I said, "she'll let go"—the second clue that I had never owned a Jack Russell! Up the great buck went, with Duchess still attached. There she hung—two feet from the cement, swinging back and forth from that buck's nose! With tightly locked jaws (a terrier specialty), she would not let go. Finally, by scratching her stomach, and talking quietly to her she dropped into my arms! (10 minutes later). Did I say something about her being afraid? I guess I was the one who got the scare!

—Gerald Bloodworth

A Hot Trip

My wife's sister's pre-wedding party was being held a half hour's drive from where we live. We were reluctant to leave for the festivity, because our adored Jack Russell Terrier, Rufus was missing. We had been looking for him all day. We had called and called, looking under bushes, in the fields, in the house, but no sign of him. It was becoming later and later, and we had to go to the party. When we left we promised ourselves we would break away early in order to continue the search. Our hearts were heavy, and although we smiled, shook hands and helped serve food and drink, our thoughts were over the Blue Ridge Mountains, 30 miles away.

We were having dinner, when a blackish terrier-type dog wandered in. My wife said "Oh, I wish it was Rufus"—Everyone looked for a few minutes, when suddenly she said "IT IS RUFUS." What a joyous reunion! But, then came the big question—How in the world had he made it to the party? We had searched the car before leaving, so we knew he hadn't traveled *IN* the car. A close examination of Rufus revealed heavy grease marks all over him and some burned hair, but no cuts of any kind. We went to examine the car, opened the hood—and there, stuck to the block, was a great collection of white hairs. Also there was a shiny spot, where he must have laid on the block for the half an hour drive. We imagined him watching Highway 50 flash under the car, while he travelled at 70 miles per hour amongst hoses, wires, whirling fans and a labyrinth of metal. But, why was he under the hood in the first place? We guessed he had been chasing his favorite varmint—a chipmunk, who with Rufus in hot pursuit, ran up into the motor. Rufus, in his enthusiasm, followed Mr. Chippy—but then couldn't figure out how to make his exit and hence went to the party in a rather unusual manner.

He survived in spite of sitting on the intensely hot engine block for over half an hour, because of his courage and tenacity which is typical of the Jack Russell Terrier. Needless to say, his thick coat contributed to saving his life.

—Tad Zimmerman

Alaskan Jack Russell

We really wanted to add a Jack Russell Terrier to our family, but were unsure whether *Alaska* was quite the right place for one. I phoned a breeder in Virginia and told her of my worries. She put my mind at ease, explaining how she had sold several Jack Russell Terriers to people living in Ontario, Canada, where it gets very cold, and they had no trouble handling the low temperatures. She did warn us the puppy probably would grow a heavier coat than usual. Further discussions led to a verbal agreement on the acquisition of a four month old, rough coated bitch, Woodluck Melba.

Excitement was high, when she finally arrived at midnight after 12 hours of air travel. She was full of life, not a bit scared, and immediately took to me. Her next two nights were spent on the couch in the den, sleeping with my wife, who didn't want her to cry or be lonely!

It is hard to believe Melba is not an Alaskan dog. She loves to be outdoors, and my wife's original idea of outfitting her with a sweater and booties was soon forgotten as she grew her own set and adapted beautifully to the cold!

She adores to go hiking with me, fishing with me and hunting for snow shoe rabbits or spruce-hen.

One day, I was hiking along a river with Melba, and I saw several freshly killed salmon. Obviously a bear was close by. I feared for Melba. We had been warned not to take a dog where there are bears. Sure enough, she went charging off—apparently on his line. Great was my relief, when I realized he was far enough ahead of us, she wouldn't meet up with him. Fearless as she is (except for the cat next door, who has her terrified!), I know she would have stood her ground.

When it comes to hunting spruce-hen, she is number one in finding these small type grouse, who are ground feeders and sit on the low branches of the trees or on the ground, camouflaged! But Melba has no problem locating them and flushing them out for me! The same is true of the snow shoe rabbits. She is small enough to burrow into the thicket or small hole, smell where they are hiding and then drive them out! They are very difficult to spot in the snow, but with my great little friend in hot pursuit, I have no trouble seeing them.

So thanks to Melba's great hunting abilities, I am way ahead of my Alaskan friends when it comes to sport in the frozen north.

Once again, the Jack Russell Terrier shows its adaptability by living, like a native, in an environment quite foreign to its breeding and background.

—Bob Eddy

"WHO'S TO BLAME?"

A postcard sent to the author's great aunt, with a postmark of 1908! Painting by Sydney Hayes.

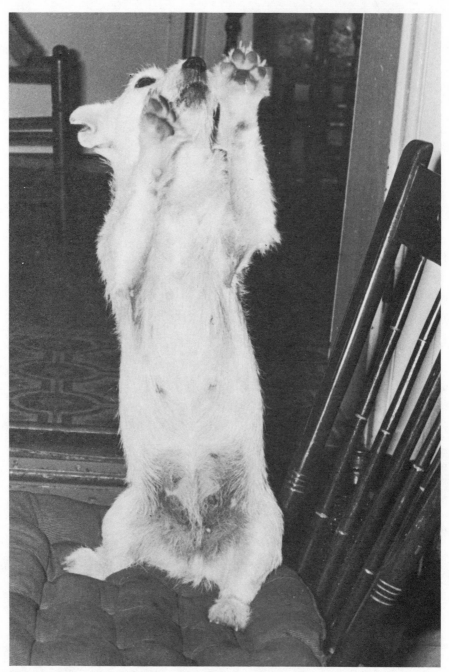

TIC-TAC is showing off her marvelous feet.

"Fan"

Fan, the hunt terrier, runs with the pack,
A little white bitch with a patch on her back;
She runs with the pack as her ancestors ran—
We're an old fashioned lot here and breed 'em like Fan;
   Round of skull, harsh of coat, game, little and low,
   The same as we bred sixty seasons ago.

   She's harder than nails, and she's nothing to learn,
from her scarred little snout to her cropped little stern,
And she hops along gaily, in spite of her size,
With twenty-four couples of big badger-pies;
   'Tis slow, but 'tis sure is the old white and grey,
   And 'twill sing to a fox for a whole winter day.

Last year at Rook's Rough, just as Ben put 'em in,
'Twan Fan found the rogue, who was curled in the whin;
She pounded his brush, with a drive and snap,
"Yip, Yap, boys," she told 'em, "I've found him, YIP-YAP";
   And they put down their noses and sung to his line
   Away down the valley most tuneful and fine.

Twas a point of ten miles and a kill in the dark,
That scared the cock pheasant in Fallowfield Park,
And into the worry flew Fan like a shot
And snatched the tit-bit that old Rummage had got;
   "Who-Whoop" Little Fan, with the patch on her back,
   She broke up the fox with the best of the pack.

—"Punch" (1900)

A Search in the Woods

While out walking with the two Jack Russells, Penny and Henri, and the German Shepherd Nikki, I came home alone as the dogs had become involved with hunting in the woods. Sometime later, Penny and Nikki returned without Henri, but I expected Henri would be along shortly. However, he still hadn't appeared a few hours later, so we set out to search for him. When we got to the woods, I watched the other two dogs carefully, and sure enough after much sniffing around they located him! I never could have found him on my own in the large woods. He had been partly buried in the hole he had been digging. The earth over him had given away and he was unable to move. All that was showing was a tiny patch of white through a small hole the size of a quarter! I dug him out, quite unharmed, and typical Jack Russell that he was, he had to be restrained from going back in!

—Lynne Westaway

(This is a common occurance, when Jack Russell Terriers dig themselves into a hole. The earth falls in behind them, and they are trapped in there. This is one of the reasons it is risky to let a terrier hunt by himself.)

A Drainful

As I listened on top of a hill, in the early morning mist, I heard hounds screaming away to the north. I jumped into my "four wheeled hunter" and tore around the block, up a farm lane, where I found hounds, staff, and a few mounted followers standing around watching something. Hounds, one or two at a time, were pushing their great heads into the 10 inch opening of a culvert, that went under the lane. Obviously, that was where Big Red was taking refuge. "How about my going back to the kennel and getting Sid Abbot's (the kennel huntsman) terriers?" I asked. Charles Kindersley, Master and huntsman of the Eglinton Hunt, Ontario, Canada, said "Splendid idea." So, off I went, with a feeling of great importance. This was 1950. I had only read about terriers and their prowess in bolting foxes and I was full of anticipation. Sid was just as enthusiastic as I was and was not about to be left behind. In a matter of minutes we were back, and Sid entered his terriers, into the culvert. The rough coated, tan headed little bitch went in first ("she's bolted many a fox") and her white son was right behind. Major Kindersley moved his hounds forty yards away. ("We must give the fox a fair chance"). He asked his field to move back, as well, and to be very quiet. As foxes are the most nervous and highly strung of all animals, any noise will cause them to sulk and hang back. Sid told me to stand still and not stomp about, for the same reason. So the stage was set and the din in the culvert was fantastic! We could hear it moving along, at a slow pace, in the direction of the other opening (some twenty feet away from where he put in the terriers). The terriers were slowly forcing our ferocious quarry in this direction; while Sid was grinning with pride—"She's a fierce one—not many foxes will face her!" It was now well over 15 minutes

A terrier's first duty is to mark fox underground for hounds. Because of many years of breeding for this purpose, they have a great affinity for hounds. They often run with a pack of fox hounds, and many times are kennelled with them.

and no fox—when all of a sudden—"he's coming out!"—and out popped a great big raccoon who raced to the first tree, ran up it—but didn't have far to climb, as it was only a five foot sapling! There he clung—swinging up and down as the small tree bent with his weight! However, the terriers were still carrying on in the culvert and after a couple of minutes, out came *another* coon, who, having more sense than coon number one (still swaying in the breeze) found a larger tree for his gateway to safety. (All this time, Major Kindersley had his hounds under complete control, and not one, even the happy-go-lucky young entry, made a move). But listen, Nipper and Tiger are *still* fighting—could it be?—Yes, it could— and last, but not least, Charles James, probably much the worse for having two coons in front of him and two crazy terriers behind him, bolted for his life. After a moment of holding hounds, Major Kindersley cheered them on, for a glorious cubhunting morning run. Sid and I took his courageous little terriers, who had challenged and bolted two coons and a fox in a 10 inch wide drain, home for a warm breakfast followed by treatment of their various bite marks and scratches.

—M.M.

Life's Terrible Beginning

My mom was a super Jack Russell Terrier. She died when she was ten years old, but was an active lady up until then. During the fortunate years I lived with her, she taught me so much. She loved to hunt and showed me all she could about hunting small game, groundhogs, and raccoons (who were her favorite).

My early puppy life was spent growing up with my family, aunts, uncles and cousins, on a beautiful farm. However, when I was three months old, I was sold to a family in New Jersey who I will call Mr. and Mrs. Z. They seemed nice enough.

The day they came to take me to their home, I felt confident my new life would be fun and enjoyable. Naturally, I hated to leave my mother but, like the terrier I was, I decided to make the best of it. As soon as we arrived at Mr. & Mrs. Z's house, I was introduced to their daughter, who was a young girl about seven years old. How wonderful, I thought—at least I will have one playmate! I soon found out the Z's knew very little about dogs and how to treat and educate them, so, in typical terrier fashion, I took great advantage of them and got away with murder. My manners were awful—I did as I pleased and wondered why they never corrected me. Mr. and Mrs.

Z led an active and social life, so I often was left in the house, with only their daughter and baby sitter. It was quite evident from the beginning, the baby-sitter "Wanda" did not take kindly to me or my terrier ways, and that is when all the trouble began. Somehow, she convinced the Zs to keep me caged up. So, my miserable life began, living in a safari crate, day after day. It was awful! I was terribly frustrated by not being able to run around and get some exercise. Daughter Z would want to play with me, but I could do nothing. She would throw a ball and I would watch it roll along the floor, or bounce off my cage. I would try to shove my nose through the bars, hoping I could at least hold it for a minute or so, and perhaps have a tug-of-war with her, but it never happened. Several times, when Wanda was busy at a job, and not paying any attention, daughter Z would sneak me out of my cage. I would take this wonderful opportunity to rush around the room, getting as much exercise as I could. It felt great to stretch my legs, and scratch my back by pushing, while I was upside down, along the carpet. It did not take long however, to "poop" out, for I was very unfit; so I would drop, curl up in a tiny ball and fall asleep on the soft carpet. All of a sudden, I would be awakened out of a sound sleep, by a swift kick, dealt to me by Wanda, and then shoved back into my prison cell. I was always frightened, shocked, and hurt, by this experience. Sometimes I would be kicked so hard, I would land several feet away from where I had been lying.

It was one of those times that finally changed my life. I remember waking up one morning, unable to move. I hurt terribly; everything hurt, even breathing. What had happened and why? It was Wanda who had done this to me. I *hated* her. For days I did not eat or move—it just hurt too much. I barely could manage to lift my head and say hello to daughter Z. For Wanda, that nasty, unkind, cruel woman, I had only a growl.

Later, I don't know how many painful days later, I was in a doctor's office with Mrs. Z. I heard her tell the doctor that I had growled at Wanda and had become very bad tempered, and what should she do about it? "Oh," said the doctor, "this terrier must have a bad temperament, and you can never correct that. I would suggest that you put him to sleep." Naturally, I did not know what he meant, but I did know I hurt terribly and wished the doctor would stop talking and do something about it. At the end of the visit, Mrs. Z seemed very upset. She grabbed me off the table and stomped out of the office. My ride home in the car was as painful as the one going to the doctor.

The following day, I found myself in the car again; but this time, the ride seemed longer. I wanted to enjoy it, for I had not had this freedom and change of scene for a long time, and I was thrilled to be out of my cage. I could not enjoy anything however, as I still hurt so badly. Every bump the car went over, felt like needles in my side. Now we were going up a long winding driveway—something seemed familiar and tugged at my instincts. A large, white washed brick house came in sight and I heard the barking of dogs, many dogs. My heart stopped for a second; for there was my mother, running up to the car as it pulled in front of the main entrance. Mrs. C came out and said "Hello" to Mrs. Z. Then, thank heavens, Mrs. Z drove away and (as I later came to realize) left my life forever. I was back home! Mom was wonderful. She came up to me right away, and showed her affection for me, by wagging her tail and giving me a few licks. Mrs. C showed her love for me by hugging me. Gosh it hurt! I tried not to show it, but could not help letting out a growl, as the pain shot through my body. She understood and did not scold me. That night, I had a lovely warm bed with a towel in it. Once again, sleeping next to my mother, I was happy for the first time since I left this home.

The next day, Mrs. C took me to the doctor. She realized I was not up to par, so I was left at the hospital for two days, and was given every test you possibly could imagine! They took blood tests and X rays, checked my teeth, and poked around everywhere. It was awful, and I did not like it one bit. However, Mrs. C finally came to pick me up. I heard the doctor tell her I apparently had been very badly treated. He found through the X rays, that my tail had been broken earlier and had set by itself. My rib was presently broken. The doctor felt these injuries could only have come from being kicked. Oh, if only I could talk! I wanted to tell them the whole awful story, so I was pleased when I gathered from what they said that they were smart enough to figure out the whole thing. On the way back to the farm, from the doctor's office, I wondered what would happen next? Would Mrs. Z be back to pick me up? Would I have to return to a life of living in that terrible cage, with that nasty woman coming to work every day? I worried about it, all the way back home.

Days, and weeks, went by, but there I was, still at my lovely farm. Mrs. Z never came back to pick me up. I have never seen her, her daughter, or Wanda again—thank goodness! Mrs. C was now my owner and I was happy once again. Oh, she is no easy mark, but at least I know where I stand with her! We get along very well, and I love being with her. She nursed me back to health and was patient with me during the days that followed, when I was regaining my confidence, and at times behaving very badly. I was afraid of people. You see, I thought anyone who put their hand down to pat me, might hit me instead, so I thought it was better to attack them first. I still am not confident with strangers, but I have learned to be a bit more patient. I really don't like people patting me—I save all my love for my family, especially Mrs. C.

—Kipper

Flying Floyd

John and I bought Floyd to be a future stud dog for our kennel. He came to us when he was five months old. Although he was very happy and playful, we didn't feel that he was particularly devoted to us, or anyone else. This was all right with us. We had bought him for breeding and hunting purposes, so we accepted that he just wanted to be himself.

Floyd had been with us for six weeks, when we went to visit some friends in Aiken, S. C. We took him along, as we thought it was a good chance for us to become better friends. I had had an accident, six months previously which had grounded me. So, when we all went riding, in the gorgeous Hitchcock Woods, it was my first ride since I had been hurt. I was so happy and light hearted—it felt marvelous to be riding again!

There are many "alleys," cut through these woods, which have lovely sandy footing. On one side are permanent jumps, made of post-and-rail, with brush at the bottom. They range in size from three to three and a half feet. The trails are so wide that you can either canter along, over the jumps, or take the path beside them. I chose the jumping route and was having a fabulous time, galloping and jumping ahead of John and our friend. I kept hearing them laughing behind me, and turned around to see what it was all about. Here comes Floyd, right behind me, jumping every jump by hurling himself in the air and clearing them without taking his eyes off me! He could easily have taken the path around the jumps, but was not about to get that far away from me! And I was worried about his devotion?

—Barbara Lowery

The "old-timers" say that when a puppy grabs hold of your hand with his front paws, it's a sign of stamina and strength.

Had 16 Year Old Kipper Gone Bonkers?

Kipper may be old, deaf, and partly blind, but he certainly is not stupid and still has an excellent nose. Upon returning from picking up the mail one morning, I found Kipper (at this point he was 16) in the house digging, if you please, in the pantry along the baseboards and trying to pull off the front of the ice machine. Thinking that he had gone bonkers, I tried to call him away, so I would not have to call in a painter and carpenter to repair the damage he was doing, at great cost to my husband, who I knew would not think kindly of the whole situation.

Nothing worked. He kept digging and carrying on no matter what I did to get him away. I finally decided to go down to the cellar to find out if there might be something down there that he was smelling. Sure enough, a huge raccoon, or possibly several raccoons, had made the cellar look like a shambles. They had gotten into everything, broken storm windows, tracked dirty, muddy feet all over, been in the coal bin, even popped into the furnace (not yet operational) and then put dirty, coal-dust paw marks all over the deep freeze, dumped a water bucket and tried to get through a drain pipe in the cellar floor which leads to the outside. What a mess!! The damage Kipper did to the baseboards and paint in the pantry was nothing compared to what the raccoons had done in the cellar. So although an old man, he still knows where it's at, and keeps me informed on the wildlife situation around our home.

—Ailsa Crawford

Hook, Line and Sinker

The Jack Russell Terrier breeder and owner is no stranger to seeing and believing the true grit and determination that makes up this tough, yet loving breed of dog.

One Sunday, my husband, a friend and I were enjoying our day of rest, sitting beside the lake where we live. It is not a super fishing lake, yet young boys find it entertaining to fish there, using cane poles and a line, with some delectable bait attached to the hook such as meat, because that is what catfish especially like. This particular day brought two neighborhood boys out, their lines baited with liver.

I was in a particularly happy mood this morning because the night before, my favorite bitch, McBean, had just presented us with seven healthy puppies (her third litter of seven!), upstairs in our bedroom. Around 1 o'clock in the afternoon, I thought it was time for a second outing since this great event, so I coaxed her from her "birthing-box," down the stairs and out onto the grass, where we were sitting. I was watching her proudly, when suddenly I saw her paw frantically scratching the side of her face, as dogs do when a stick is caught between their teeth. I called her to come to me, and as she came, I noticed to my horror, she was dragging one of the poles. Apparently, when the boys had gone to lunch, they had left their poles, liver bait still on the hooks, lying on the bank. Naturally, McBean couldn't resist such a tender morsel—and now my poor dog was definitely attached to the pole, by means of the line! Closer inspection showed no signs of the hook or sinker. Was it caught in her throat? Had it passed to her stomach? Was it caught in her intestines? We immediately made five phone calls, and finally located our vet, Danny Culbreth, who agreed to meet us at his office right away. With poor McBean still attached to the line, (we had cut it away from the pole and I was holding it as still as possible so as not to move the swallowed hook), we rushed to the clinic.

Danny, realizing the seriousness of the situation, had called in his assistant (who had to leave a family dinner in the country). They took x-rays (I have them to this day) which showed that the hook, liver and sinker, were still attached to the line and were in her stomach! The operation, to remove them, was made even more difficult than usual, as McBean was so swollen with milk.

Once the operation was finished and was pronounced successful, my next thought was what about the puppies? The vet, Danny, warned that it would be at least two to three hours before she would be able to navigate at all, so she must be kept away from the puppies. Also, we were told not to let her nurse them for two days, to assure that the stitches would hold. On the way home, we stopped at a farm where we picked up some goat's milk to feed the puppies.

We laid poor, almost unconscious McBean on her doggie bean bag, downstairs and then tackled our next chore—feeding the goat's milk to the puppies (still in our bedroom, upstairs) with an eye dropper! Ten minutes into the process of coaxing the tiny fellows to accept the dropper, my husband and I were dumbfounded, as we heard some bumping noises on the stairs, followed by a very drunk McBean coming through our bedroom door, staggering from side to side, bumping first into the chest of drawers, then into the bed, then into the closet doors, finally lifting her front paws up into the hole in the cardboard box where the puppies were, and then, literally throwing herself into it. She never touched one, as she slumped down amongst them—and passed out again. Up to this point, we had not been able to speak, as we watched this courageous act by our gutsy little mother—something having told us to let her do what she was compelled to do. We both decided right then, if her instinct was that strong, even under such heavy medication, she deserved the right to stay with her puppies; besides which, we didn't have the heart to interfere with our determined little trouper.

(McBean stayed with the puppies—the operation had not slowed the milk supply—the stitches held and she raised all seven without any further help from us.)

—Leslie Large

"a very drunk McBean......"

The Jack Russell Terrier as Nursemaid

Everyone who is involved with Jack Russell Terriers is familiar with their hallmark character traits: intelligent, brave, loyal, alert, affectionate, and so on. But recent events at my house have brought to light another trait, "the Jack Russell Terrier as Nursemaid."

My husband Jeffrey had suffered a severely broken leg, leaving him on crutches, with a cast from hip to toe. He was confined to the house—or to be more exact, to the living room couch. Since I work and would be gone all day, I worried how he and Jeb, our 11 month old Jack Russell Terrier puppy, would make out together. Jeb's certainly not bad, but he *is* active. Anyone lying on the couch is usually "fair game" for a springing attack with his toy—Jeb's way of saying "Let's play!"

However, from the minute Jeffrey arrived home from the hospital, Jeb began an astounding metamorphosis, from a rowdy little puppy, into an A#1 nursemaid and companion. He would, oh-so-carefully, hop onto the couch (instead of his usual leap), and carefully lie by Jeffrey's side, sometimes resting his head on the cast. Jeb would stay there for hours. His movements around Jeffrey became almost feline as he tip-toed around. Anywhere Jeffrey went, he had as an escort, a little dog with a furrowed brow and a look of deep concern on his face.

There was none of the monkey business of barking to go out, or to come in, or yipping for a biscuit, or any of the usual "nudginess' of a young dog. Jeb had become more protective of us and remained on "high alert" for any strange sounds around the house.

I thought the biggest problem for Jeffrey would be getting Jeb to come in from outside. Jeb has been know to be somewhat selective in whether or not he hears someone calling him when he's busy in the great outdoors. Jeffrey could only call him from the back porch. As it turned out, Jeb was *not* the problem; our very sweet and dear 13 year old Golden Retriever, Rover, was. Not because she's disobedient, but because she is almost deaf! Jeffrey could yell himself hoarse and she still wouldn't come to him. That's when the puppy stepped in. The dogs were well off from the house when Jeffrey began calling. Jeb stopped and looked up, but Rover just ambled along, oblivious to any sound. Suddenly, Jeb ran to Rover, jumped up and nipped her ear twice, and started for the house. This induced Rover to look up and see Jeffrey, and quickly follow the puppy home.

I must admit I doubted Jeb's intentions until I saw the performance repeated the next evening. This time Jeb did two quick laps around Rover to get her attention and started for home, with Rover right behind.

The curious thing is that Jeb won't do this if he knows I'm at home; I've only seen this performance when he doesn't know I'm there. Evidently, if I'm home I'm in charge of Rover, and when I'm gone, he takes over the responsibility!

—Beth Carnes

Rita King

Who's There?

When I went to live and work in Washington, D.C., my mother was worried about my personal safety, as I would be living alone. I had rented the smallest house in Georgetown, 2 rooms downstairs, living-room at the front, kitchen area at the back, and a bedroom and bathroom upstairs. I did have as my roommate my trusty Jack Russell Terrier, WOODLUCK SLURPY, but that didn't assuage my mother's fears. So for my protection she bought a gorgeous German Shepherd female puppy. Nisha was a saint and made many believers of the gentleness of the German Shepherd as a breed. We were quite a trio as we walked (or I rode my bicycle) through the streets of Georgetown. The two dogs were sidewalk trained and both would wait at the curb for my permission to cross the road etc. It was a riot in the park—I trained them to teeter-totter with each other; they both could climb the ladder and slide down the slide— and best of all, they loved the flat wheel that spun around and around. All this was fine—but I was never sure that Nisha was the watch dog and protector my mother envisioned.

One night it looked like I was going to find out—It was 2 o'clock in the morning, when I was awakened by a noise downstairs in my living room. I was petrified! *Now,* I was pleased to have Nisha. She slept at the head of the stairs, so I knew any minute, she would set off the alarm. I tiptoed out of bed, clutched Slurpy and headed for the stairs. What a wonderful watch dog I had—Nisha looked up at me, wagged her tail and went back to sleep—thanks, a lot, Nisha! Still clutching Slurpy, heart thumping so loudly I knew the intruder could hear it, I crept down the stairs. I *did* have a watch dog though—Slurpy was growling a deep throated growl—some comfort anyway. The light switch was at the bottom of the stairs, so my plan was to drop Slurpy and throw the light on at the same time. By saying "Rats" to him, I knew I could at least count on him taking a good bite at my unwelcome guest. It worked fine—Slurpy left me with a roar, the lights blared on, and I said with a real stage voice "WHAT DO YOU WANT?" Slurpy took off across the room and grabbed my adversary! Imagine my astonishment when—you'd never guess—he proudly trotted back to me with a huge possum hanging out of either side of his mouth!

When I finally collected my wits and could speak again, I ordered Slurpy to drop the possum, which he did. I did feel badly when I saw he had killed it—but I had to sit down and have a good laugh—and of course, apologise to Nisha, who had known more than Slurpy and me. Even though it was now 2:30 in the morning I had to share my excitement with someone, so I called Mum and told her the story. She was a sport and we had a good laugh. When I explained that Slurpy had KILLED the possum, she laughed even harder. Slightly put out, I asked her what was so funny about that. She replied "The possum's not dead—it's playing *possum!*" That was an even worse thought. How was I going to get it out of the house? Mum suggested going to bed and letting the possum worry about that, but I really didn't think I could go to sleep with a possum wandering around downstairs. "O.K., then pick him up by his tail, and he'll just hang as if he's dead, and you can put him in the

..... with a huge possum hanging out of either side of his mouth."

garden," she told me. I followed her directions, but she forgot to mention to pick him up by the END of his tail! I got hold of the tail too close to his body and he immediately wrapped it tightly around my wrist. I ran outside—but as hard as I shook my arm, he wouldn't let go—UGH! Again, Slurpy came to the rescue—he grabbed him and once more the possum "died." Slurpy carried him down the steps and deposited him in the garden! That was the last we ever saw him.

Nisha, many times, provided to be a good watch dog when people were involved, while Slurpy took care of the varmints as well as helping Nisha at guard duty.

—Denya

"Bandit is a healthy, happy dog. His best friend is our other dog "Mopey," a mutt who lives up to his name. You could really allow your imagination to run wild, picturing how these two get along. They are comic, to say the least, hilarious at times. One moment Bandit will rile "Mopey" to his height of anger, and the next, they will be sleeping together on their doggie bean bag."

Turner, Come Home

I am a blacksmith by trade. My hobbies are riding, point-to-point racing, foxhunting and raising Jack Russell Terriers. We live in the east foothills of the Blue Ridge Mountains but my job, very often, takes me across these mountains, into Warren and Clarke counties. My constant companion is Turner, a rough coated, twelve inch tall terrier. He is well known in Northern Virginia and is welcome at the stables where I shoe horses, as he spends his time, while I'm shoeing, in hunting down the resident rats and mice. Fighting is an unknown word to him—he loves everyone and their dogs!

One day, when Turner was eight years old, we went to have lunch with a friend, who lives on a mountain farm, eight and a half miles off the main road. After our visit, as I was getting into my truck to leave for a very crowded afternoon of shoeing, his German Shepherd dog escaped from the house and fiercely attacked Turner. It was unexpected and savage. Turner tried to defend himself, but the odds were too heavily stacked against him. By the

Three HARD SAUCE children, out of different bitches.

hardest, we broke the German Shepherd off Turner, who immediately ran into the mountain. I had a quick glimpse of him as he disappeared and noticed his left side had been ripped open. It was two o'clock; I immediately forgot my afternoon appointments. For three and a half hours I searched and called for Turner, but finally had to call an end to the hunt, as it was becoming too dark in the densely wooded mountain, to be able to see anything. I left my sweater and jacket on the ground, not too near the house, as I knew Turner would be afraid of the German Shepherd, even though I had been assured by my friend that he would keep his dog shut up. Leaving a piece of clothing on the ground is a night hunter's trick—they do this when their hounds don't "come in" from the night hunt and they can't wait for them any longer. When the hound does return, he lies on the clothing, knowing his owner will be back to get him. I went to the mountain, searching and calling for him, everyday for five days, but then I reluctantly gave up and presumed he was dead.

In the meantime, my friend had the local radio station broadcast, several times a day, the information about a missing, wounded terrier in the Front Royal area.

Exactly a week to the day, I was listening to the radio on my way to work, when I heard the local station report a small tan and white terrier type, male dog had been seen. They said this dog had been hurt, was scared and no one could get near him. Two minutes later, I was in a phone booth, dialing the number given by the radio station. The man who answered gave me directions to his place, but my hopes were not very high as he lived so far away from where I had last seen Turner. However, when I met the man, his description of the dog he had befriended, by leaving water and feed out for him, certainly sounded like Turner, wounds and all. I walked up, into the Blue Ridge Mountains in the direction the man had last seen him go, and sat down on a rock to call and wait. With a heavy heart, I hollered his name and then blew a long note on my copper hunting horn. Incredibly and wonderfully, it wasn't very long before I heard the weeds rustling. Through my tear clouded eyes, I was barely able to recognise my friend as he dragged himself towards me, trying to wag his short tail. He was hardly able to move, his coat was completely plastered with blood and dirt, and worst of all his whole body was covered with blood-sucking ticks. The temperatures that week had been in the high ninties and there had been no rain. He had survived, with little or no water and feed only because of his tremendous courage and his driving force to get home to safety and help. He had travelled eighteen miles; had crossed both the North and the South fork of the Shenandoah River (each one at least 100 yards wide); had crossed an interstate highway; had traversed the city (20,000) of Front Royal; and now he was very deep in the Blue Ridge Mountains and was halfway to the top of them. From where he had been attacked he was moving in a straight line towards home. When we found each other he still had ten miles to go, which would have meant crossing over the top of the Blue Ridge mountains, into our valley far below.

Turner completely recovered, with lots of T.L.C. from my whole family—and to-day, at 11 years old, is just as tough and handsome as he ever was!

—Jim Magee

The Big Dig

Monday afternoon, about five o'clock, I was walking around our new place with my terriers Tara and her brother Kipper, enjoying a breath of fresh air, and relaxing away from desk work. All of a sudden, Kipper took off into the woods. A few minutes later, I heard a barking, quite deep underground and the next thing I knew, Tara was running to the rescue. From past experience, I knew what was going to happen, so I ran after her, calling madly for her to come back. In good Jack Russell Terrier style, she paid absolutely no attention what-so-ever, and continued on her merry way towards the excitement. A few minutes later, I hear *two* Jack Russells barking, deep in the bowels of the earth!! Realizing there was absolutely nothing I could do, I went back to the house and left them to do their thing, whatever that was. I hoped they would get bored and come home when night fell. Knowing Jack Russells as I do, I should have realized they would never get bored and they would be there, as long as the raccoon was there. When darkness came, my husband and I could hear the terriers barking and a bull raccoon growling, all through the drain pipes, inside and outside of the house. We feebly tried to call the terriers out again, with no luck. Then we started digging in a pipe close to the house. Upon reaching the pipe, several drinks later, we found it was too small for the terriers or coon, and even though we could still hear them, we obviously had the wrong pipe and our efforts had been in vain. Exhausted, we wished them well and went to bed!

"Here it is cocktail time, and they still haven't found our cousins!"

The following morning, there were no dogs, no noises, no coons, only absolute silence. We called and called at the entrance to the pipe, which we had located in the woods, and from far, far, far, away came barking; but only for a few seconds. It was evident the terriers and raccoon had travelled quite some distance during the night; but in what direction and where? Now what to do?

We could not leave them in the pipe. Kipper, being the one to enter first, was obviously trapped between the coon at one end and his sister, Tara, at the other. If he was seriously injured by the raging raccoon, or was not getting enough air, due to being sand-wiched in the middle, he probably would die. I could not stand the thought. He was my constant buddy and friend. He had lived through the fire (that had burned our house to the ground a few months earlier) by jumping out a second floor window, 30 feet down, with me. I had to go after him, no matter what.

The local back-hoe was called in immediately. At eight o'clock Tuesday morning, the digging began. We followed the eight inch pipe all the way through the woods, breaking into it from time to time to listen for the terriers, or to see if we could spot them. We kept digging and digging and digging and digging. Neighbors who passed by, wondered if I was building a new house. Even our local huntsman began to give up hope. People we didn't know appeared on the scene, until finally a dozen or more were all standing around shaking their heads. I feel sure they were thinking I should be put in the local "nut-house"!! My husband, getting discouraged at the mess on our lovely lawn, which now looked like a World War I trench, took off for his business in New York. The back-hoe men, who kept mentioning he had never been on a job that took him so long, was kept going with pats on the back, beers and man sized sandwiches, which he devoured as if he were never going to eat again! Time was running out, as it was becoming dark. The weath-erman had forecasted rain and stormy conditions. The front was starting to move through.

At 4:45 Tuesday evening, after the back-hoe had been digging, non-stop, for ten hours, making a trench four hundred feet long and ten feet deep, Tara, Kipper and the raccoon popped out of the end of the pipe! All three of them had been together in that drain pipe for over 24 hours!

When I went into the house to bath the dogs and treat Kipper for a few bad lacerations of the gum and inside of his mouth, I disco-vered we had no phone, no water and no lights, because all lines had been cut by the back-hoe! I first took care of the terriers, then quickly rallied around to call in the necessary people to fix us up, before my husband came home. I knew if he realized the situation, he would turn around in the driveway and drive out again!! I am pleased to say that all ended well. My husband still loved me and the terriers (inspite of the bill for this operation)! Kipper and Tara were no worse for wear, and the trench was completely filled in and seeded with lawn seed. I might add, a screen was put over the end of the drain, hopefully to prevent this from happening again.

I guess this is one of the best raccoon tales—depending on which side of the fence you are sitting on. You can rest assured that for my husband and myself, it was a total disaster and hardly a laughing matter! At that stage in our life, we could have put the cost of the whole operation to a much better use, like buying furniture for the new house etc. But who can resist a Jack Russell Terrier??

—Ailsa Crawford

SHEER'S J.R., waiting for his daily ride! He is owned by Susan Miranti, Long Island, New York.

WALNUT owned by Lynn Westaway, Ontario, Canada. This bitch is an excellent type. She stands 13½ inches, has a grand head, neck and shoulder. Her body is flat but she has enough depth through the girth for ample lung room, has a strong back line and super straight legs. Notice how low set her knees and hocks are, and how wide and flat the gaskin is.

"......I found myself climbing up after him"

Long Island is a Blast for Me

Like all Jack Russell Terriers, I have a thought a minute—and get restless if my human Mom doesn't let me stretch my imagination outside. Fortunately for me, she's a great sport and loves to do different things. We live on Long Island, so unlike many of my Jack Russell cousins, I don't have the opportunity to do much hunting. But, boy, do I have fun. We have these marvelous grey furry things in our backyard, which have huge bushy tails, and can run like crazy. (I think they are called squirrels.) They had me beaten, for awhile, by tearing up the first tree they came to. One day, one made me so furious, I found myself climbing up after him. I have now perfected my technique. I wrap my front legs around the tree and with the help of my dew claws, which do the pulling and my hind feet, which do the pushing, I can shinny right up behind him. So far, I have only tasted his tail—but someday, he'd better watch out!

Mom has a funny looking thing, with only two wheels. She loves to ride this and one day, don't ask me why, I decided I wanted to go along—so I jumped into the seat in which her daughter usually rides and off we went. I don't know why everyone looks at us and has a laugh. Seems quite normal to me! Oh well!

We often go to a nearby place (all of us—Mom, daughter and I) where there are all kinds of fun things for the daughter to do. Mom throws a ball for me—which I love—I tear after it, try to kill it (it just won't die) bring it back to Mom and we start again. One day, while I was working off steam doing this, daughter was walking up some very steep stairs (I think she called it a ladder) and then with squeals of delight sailed down the other side, on her bottom. Suddenly I thought—"Why not me" so before Mom could say "Boo!" I had climbed the ladder (a little tricky) and had slid down the other side—More darn fun! I do this a lot now. I think Mom gets as much kick out of it as I do.

I remember a day Mom seemed especially pleased with me. We were all walking beside a lake, when we came up to two rather sad looking boys. Mom, who is really nice to everyone, asked them what was wrong. They pointed to a bobbin, floating in the lake. Their fishing line had broken and they were losing this thing, as it bobbed away. "Don't worry" said Mom and called me for a game. She threw a rock (I guess that's what it was) and I joyfully jumped into the lake and swam to the splash. I couldn't find anything that had her hand smell on it, so settled for this other thing, which was bouncing around in the water and brought it back to her. She gave it to the boys, and I gave myself a good shake. We then continued on our way, leaving the two open mouthed boys to continue their fishing.

So, you see, us lucky Jack Russells can have a great time, even though we live in a built-up area, if we have a fun Mom like mine.

—Shor's J.R.

The City's Not For Jack

Jack, who was living in the city, adored going to the farm. Any mention of a trip to it in the offing, had him hanging around underfoot, terrified we might forget and leave without him. One day my brother was preparing to come to the farm, using my parents' new car. To make sure Jack would be around when he was ready to leave, he told him he was going to the farm (or perhaps he said f.a.r.m. as Jack had even learned to spell his favourite word). However, at departure time, Jack was nowhere to be found. After spending some time searching and calling, he had to leave without him. As there was no one left in the city house, we made repeated calls over the next two days to the neighbors, who were kindly looking for him; but there was no sign of Jack. Finally, I thought to ask someone to check inside the older car, left in the garage, even though the garage itself had been checked several times. There they found Jack, sitting on the back seat, patiently waiting to go to the farm!

(Jack's love of the country did not go unrewarded. Shortly after this he said goodbye to his city friends and moved to the farm!)

—Lynne Westaway

I Want To Be Alone

When Dolly had her first litter of puppies, we allowed her to be in the house, although she normally lives outside (by her own choice). Apparently, this did not suit her too well, which she emphasized by chewing furniture, scratching the rugs and generally showing her frustrations. So when her second litter was on its way, I fixed a pen for her and her puppies and in one corner I built a cozy kennel with a heat lamp to keep it warm. We put her in it for a few days, before the puppies came, to give her time to accept it as her new home and be happy there. She seemed pleased and took it on as her place.

HARD SAUCE and TAMALE after a chase in the ocean.

"You can't fool us—we know you're making supper!" Five noses belonging to Lynn Wade's (Florida) terriers.

A special coat for Mr. & Mrs. Bob Eddy's terrier, WOOD LUCK MELBA, who grew it for her Alaskan home.

In 1899 the American artist John M. Tracy painted these hunt terriers marking a rock break. Notice the similarity to the terriers in the photo on page 165.

Ailsa Crawford's famous KIPPER.

A charming painting by Nola L. McConna, Toronto, Canada.

W. H. Trood, 1900.

Some of the Fernie dog pack in with a hunt terrier.
anon., circa 1890.

Six beautiful puppies arrived on time and all was fine for the first two days—when, on the morning of the third day—there was no sign of mother or children. We looked everywhere. Finally, as almost a last resort, I looked in my workshop. I couldn't believe what I saw—Dolly was there with all her beautiful, previously white puppies laid out on a bed of coals!! She had carried them out of the pen (but how?), jumped up three feet through the window and down a drop of three feet. She had taken a bag of coal, somehow ripped it open, and then made a lovely bed of black coals for her and her puppies to lie on.

The family was immediately moved back into the pen. I was curious as to how she had achieved this; but thought no more about it, until later that day, bless me, if the family hadn't moved a second time to the bed of coals! Again I put them back in the pen and this time I decided to watch them. For awhile nothing happened. Finally (she didn't see me looking!) Dolly picked up a puppy in her mouth, went to the corner of the pen, where I had put a box to cover up a hole in the fence, jumped on the box, over the fence and through the window, into my workshop. She did this with another one, but when she started off with number three, she turned around and caught me looking at her. Like a child caught in the act of cookie-stealing, she quietly dropped back and put the puppy down! At this point, I decided, that for whatever reason, she was determined to have her puppies lying on bumpy coal in a rather draughty workshop. So, with a sigh of resignation, I put a heavy horse blanket over the coals, and let her stay where she wanted to be.

This worked well for three more days—but then the family disappeared once more! A thorough search found them under the barn! We had quite a struggle to get them out, because they were so far underneath. That did it! She is now trapped in the kitchen. Whether she likes it or not *we* do. Dolly's determination to hide herself and her family from us, must stem from an old instinct compelling the mother and her pups to "den" away from predators and danger.

—Ray Carter

(Dolly comes from a long line of working terriers who hunt with foxhound packs. She runs with the Newmarket (Maryland) hounds, never missing a day's hunting, and often, through her terrier skills, provides more sport for the mounted hunt followers. She was grand champion Terrier at the Virginia Foxhound Club Hound Show in 1983 and 1984.)

Sir Jocelyn Lucas Says . . .

. . . Another point about hunt terriers in different parts of the country, is that they are not always used with the same idea. With the vast majority of packs, they are not meant to kill foxes at all, but to bolt them. A terrier that is put into an earth and kills his fox would be regarded as worse than a nuisance, for he might easily ruin a day's sport. They are meant to provide foxes, in fact to provide a hunt, if necessary, and not to kill or hurt the fox. The Reverend Jack Russell, whose terriers have achieved immortality, used to say that he wanted his dogs to worry and tease the fox till he bolted, to keep yapping at him so that the diggers could know where to work, but never to "mix things."

—Sir Jocelyn Lucas, M.C.M.P
Hunting and Working Terriers

"I could see why you were reluctant to part with Snap. She is so perfect—what a little package. She has endeared herself to everyone here, especially me. I love her."

No Better Friend than a Jack Russell Terrier

Percy a Chihuahua, and Mick a Jack Russell Terrier, lived in a market town in Yorkshire, England. They were great friends, even though they had different homes. One day, Percy was hit by a car, and his owner, after making certain there was no heart beat and seeing his glazed, unfocused eyes, knew he had been killed. She put him in a burlap sack and sadly buried him in her garden.

Hours later, his Jack Russell friend Mick, came by for the daily frolic. Not finding him, he searched the garden. Almost immediately he located his playmate's grave and started digging frantically. He came to the sack, dug it out and dragged it towards the house. Rather upset, the parents of the owner of Percy ran outside to stop Mick. However, on examination they found Percy still alive! He was pretty shakey and feeble, but a few days later he was back to his old self! How did Mick know his friend was alive? He knew because he was a Jack Russell Terrier, that's how.

Did McBean Make It?

After a visit with her sister Caroline in Berryville, Va., Leslie got ready to start the long drive back to her home in Thomasville, Georgia, accompanied by her 3 year old daughter, Delia. However, she was becoming very apprehensive about starting the trip, because another passenger in the car was her Jack Russell terrier bitch WOODLUCK McBEAN, who although she was due to whelp in a few days, was giving all the indications of whelping early. After much kidding and debate, Leslie decided to make a run for it. Delia was cautioned to leave Beannie alone etc. etc. The trip was going famously. Delia was behaving beautifully when, after a long silence she said, "Mummy, I don't feel well." Leslie quietly despaired and wondered what to do as thoughts of car sickness flashed through her mind. Suddenly, Delia again broke the silence with "I'm going to have puppies!" (Beannie made it to Thomasville and had 7 puppies a few days later.)

—M.M.

WOODLUCK BLINTZ

Rat Patrol

It's led by a terrier with the canines of an
alligator and a grudge against rodents

Kenneth James

I purchased my dairy farm in south-central Pennsylvania in 1972. Along with several hundred acres, a herd of Holstein cattle and equipment, I also bought a wellstocked rat colony. By 1974, the rats on my farm had bred up a vast population, and that's when I learned about fighting rats.

The damage the rats were causing, was unbelievable. I had to grind an extra 500 pounds of cattle feed every two weeks to ensure that I would have enough for the cows and the rats. The bottom four feet of the corncrib looked like a bomb had exploded there; every cob of corn was stripped clean. Feedbags were ruined; the walls and floors of the barns had rat holes chewed in them; even the cinderblock walls had rat holes. Two things finally made me take action. First, I learned of a neighboring farmer who had lost several cows to leptospirosis due to diseased rats. However, the clincher was the appalling sensation when I walked into the unlit barn, from a multitude of rats squeaking and rushing past my legs and above my head. So I went to war.

The hostilities begin with a visit to the local feedstore where I buy several pounds of the latest superduper rat poison. That evening I set out bags of poison around all the runs and holes I can find, and go to bed expecting to find great swarms of sick and dying rats in a few hours. The next morning, every bag of poison has been partially buried or used by the rats as a latrine. I can see that I have vastly underrated my opponents. Not eating the poison is bad enough, but to warn the other members of the colony by urinating and defecating on the bags is a bit insulting.

My mistake, I conclude, came introducing a strange food to the rats, so I mixed a different type of poison together with cow feed and ground corn. The next day, confident of a good kill, I am met instead with the same situation. My estimation of the rat's intelligence goes up about 100 per cent, while the estimation of my own falls accordingly.

I explain my problem to the county agricultural agent, and he tells me of a poison that rats can't resist. Well, he's wrong. By that time I have about $125 worth of poison, either partially buried or being used as a bathroom by goodness knows how many rats. The year 1974 ends with the rats winning the war.

The early spring of 1975 turns out to be a banner season for rat breeding. I think if poisons won't work, maybe natural predation is the answer. I agree to take all the cats at the humane society. I pick up fifteen cats of all shapes and sizes. Maybe I have a chance.

For several weeks, I actually think the cats are doing their job. Damage to feed is just as great, but I don't see any live rats in the morning. I don't see any dead rats either! Maybe the cats are eating them? However, they sure haven't lost their appetite for milk! The damage continues, and I have a sinking feeling that the rats are lying low. My fears are soon confirmed. While mucking out a calf stall, I dislodge a rat, napping next to the feed pan. Out the stall door he goes, with me in hot pursuit, swinging a shovel and shouting profanities. The rat veers down the feedway and cuts towards another door. I realize its path will take it striaght into fifteen sets of razor-sharp teeth and piercing claws, which are lying in a pile by the milk bowl. The rat barrels into the cats, makes a leap sideways, and shoots out the door. Fifteen cats get up, look around, stretch, lick their paws, and go back to sleep.

Later, I walk into the grain room, to find my big yellow tomcat, backed into a corner, with a rat a couple of inches from his face. That afternoon, I loaded up all the cats for a trip back to the humane society.

My next idea is blacksnakes. I catch ten and turn them loose under the corncrib, and that's the last I see of them. The rats probably had them for breakfast.

By now it's become almost worth my life to walk into the feed room. The rats don't even run any more; they sort of amble out of my way.

My next plan of attack is traps. I buy a fancy type that allows several rats to get in, but not out. I set the $15 trap in the grain room, and the next morning I find the cage holding six squealing rats. Four years, and my first victory! But, the trap never catches another rat, no matter where I set it or how I camouflage it. I have a very intelligent colony of rats.

Next I try a device like a mousetrap, but fifty times bigger. Its spring would wound a bear. I bait ten traps with peanut butter; but the next morning all ten are sprung and the peanut butter licked clean. But no rats. Thinking it must have been luck, I set all the traps again. The next morning, all are sprung, with no rats in them. Not being a fast learner, I use up a whole jar of crunchy peanut butter before I realize I've been outsmarted again. My rats are not only intelligent, they're athletic, too—I give up.

Sometimes the gods on high smile down on us poor suckers. Three years later, my brother and his wife came for a weekend visit. Traveling with them was one of the mongreliest-looking dogs I had ever seen. She was small, about ten inches at the shoulders, had a white body with brown patches, and a mouth that looked as if it belonged on an alligator—canines so long that they protruded below her upper lip.

I start razzling my brother about this strange looking pet. I'm told it's a Jack Russell terrier—they are good for bolting foxes, going to ground on woodchucks, and are excellent rat killers. I immediately drag my brother, his wife, and the dog, Eve, to the corncrib, thinking, "If this creature can kill a rat, I'll eat it." How thankful I am, a few minutes later, that I didn't say it out loud.

Eve, having spent the first eleven months of her life in an apartment has never seen a rat and so has never been blooded. She prances over to the corncrib, sniffs once and then gives out a bloodcurdling bark, scream, yip—take your choice. I move a board lying by the crib and out scamper two rats. All Eve's instincts click about two seconds late, and the rats get away. But light bulbs are going off in my head like the Las Vegas Strip.

The next mark is a clump of hay. I kick it aside, and Eve moves as I never knew anything could. She catches the rat, and the noise of its death throes fills the air—music to my ears. We kill two more rats. Unfortunately my sister-in-law does not like Eve getting all that blood on herself, so we have to quit.

My brother left the next day, but swore he would locate a Jack Russell for me. A few days later, I receive a phone call from him, telling me that Eve had flipped her lid, and can I take her? After her first kill, her personality changed drastically. She chewed the furniture, tried to disembowel a neighbor's cat, attacked my brother, but the crowning feat was depositing her morning business on the kitchen table. Eve was dropped on my doorstep the next day and we got down to business.

Eve and I begin a hunt that is to last four months. I decide to start at the outer perimeter of the farm buildings and work in. The first building is the equipment shed. Eve immediately marks the culti-packer. I jab a stick down one end, while Eve stands at the other. Eight rats bolt out of Eve's end. Two are caught, and the other six scatter. Eve trails one to a corner where is is hiding under a board. Eve locates; I lift board; Eve kills rat.

A partner that hates rats more than I do is almost too good to be true. Next we go to the baler; Eve clambers around it, barking. I lift her into the baler, and she quickly scampers back into the chamber. It's a dead end for the rats. Eve kills four, and I get one as it tries to escape. By afternoon we have killed thirty rats. Eve's tongue is hanging down to her toes. She stills wants more, and is downright angry when I quit.

The next day we head back to the machine shed to finish where we left off. But we have to start all over again, as Eve marks every place we hunted yesterday. The cultipacker yields up three more rats. There are rats in the baler, rats in the mower, rats in the harvester. Twenty more rats killed. The last machine to be hunted has an auger with two doors hinged on it. Eve says there is a rat in there, I lift the door, and Eve squeezes her way to the rat. I hear the rat squeal, and then Eve yelps. This rat, the first to have bitten her, is her toughest adversary, so far, but Eve dispatches it, and we call it a day. Fifty rats in two days!

I was worried that Eve's bite might put her off rats, but she proved more determined than ever. All week we spent three to four hours a day killing rats. Rats were everywhere—under boards, under hay, under tin, under just about everything that didn't move. The rats we killed were huge. For the next several months Eve was like the Grim Reaper. She made her rounds every day and let me know if she needed assistance. The approximate tally for the year was 600 adult and 200 immature rats.

Since that first memorable hunt, I have owned several more Jack Russells. I've found that it takes a continuing effort to keep a place free of rats. One pair can, conceivably, have some thousands of descendants in a year's time. An average litter numbers around a dozen, and a rat is sexually mature at about twelve weeks.

My farm is rat-free approximately four months out of the year, but after the first frost in the fall, the rats start moving in. Their favorite hiding place is in the haymow under 10,000 bales of hay. The dogs have a difficult time getting at the rats there, and it's usually not until spring, when most of the hay is gone, that we

EVE

manage to roust them out. My dogs typically kill between 300 to 500 rats a year. I've heard it estimated that one rat costs a farmer $20 a year in damages. So you can see, my Jack Russell Terriers really are worth their weight in gold.

(Kenneth James lives on a dairy farm with his wife, three children, six Jack Russells, and a decreasing colony of worried rats.)

Beth Carnes' Jeb keeps in top shape, mentally and physically, through strenuous ball games in his back yard.

A stick also provides terriers with a great deal of exercise in a short time.

The rats win the battle against the cats!

Nothing stops us! WOODLUCK BOING and WOODLUCK TAMALE.

LADY DEVON OF DEVONSHIRE owned by Mr. and Mrs. Kent Gemmel, New Hampshire.

Practical Advice
& Training

What is a Suitable Home for a Jack Russell Terrier

The characteristic that sets the Jack Russell Terrier apart from other breeds is his ADAPTABILITY. It is this one personality trait that has made him so popular with horsemen, who are often "on-the-move" with different living situations from one week to the next. No matter where you go or what you are busy doing, he trots along cheerfully, happy to be with you, and all the time keeping an eye and ear on the look-out for some fun—ready to join in what ever might be on the agenda next!

As a breeder, I have sold Jack Russell Terriers into many different types of homes, and they all seem to have worked out well. The anecdotes in this book tell of terriers in many different situations and homes, proving their adaptability. There are two things that are a MUST for a Jack Russell home—he *must* be with people a great deal of his waking time, and there must be, at least once a week, a time where he can be out, with someone who will watch him to see where he goes, satisfying his hunting instincts, his digging compulsions and his love of running free. There is no reason why he cannot be left alone, for the eight to nine hours while his family works, *provided* the rest of the day he has company which would include a long walk, a run in the park, a wild game of chase the ball, a tug of war etc. Then, as mentioned, a time on the weekend when he gets a free run in the country, or some such place. What would be completely unfair, would be a city environment, where he was always on a leash and never had any freedom from one week to the next. For this home, he is completely unsuitable. Nor, by the same token, is he a lap dog for an elderly person, who can never take him out or who doesn't have someone to play with him. In other words, he can be a city dog, owned by a working person for five days a week—providing at least one, or even better, both of the other two days allow him to follow his inherited instincts.

The same applies to selling a puppy into a kennel life. To say he can live in a kennel with other terriers from one day to the next, with little human association but can't live in a place where he is by himself for eight to nine hours a day, is senseless. These dogs have far too much personality to live with only dogs for company—they have to have the relationship with people—people who show them sport and fun. So given the choice, the terrier would choose the apartment life as outlined above, to the life in a kennel, with little human attention.

What about a home with young children? Here again, it depends on the situation. It the children are watched while the dog is with them, I think it is great for both parties. They love to play together, and bringing up "the young" to respect and love animals, is marvelous training and of course the puppy (soon to be dog) adores the companionship. I honestly believe, that there are very few children, who having been properly taught, would intentionally hurt a puppy or kitten. As for myself, a great black Newfoundland dog brought up me and my sister and brother. He went everywhere with us and we adored him. I don't think, to the best of my memory, we ever did one thing to hurt him.

The suitable home for a Jack Russell Terrier is one where he has human companionship a great deal of the time, and a safe place to run and hunt at least one or two days a week. However, I must emphasize that because of his tremendous imagination, he needs supervision when he is running to keep him from getting into dangerous situations and to be there to help him if he does.

"The dogs are beautiful and have become a great addition to our family."

Jack Russell Terrier puppies and young people have a wonderful affinity for each other. The Jack Russell makes a marvelous playmate for the only child. Needless to say, this requires supervision and direction from an adult.

"Who needs a teddy bear?"

Choosing Your Puppy

I find it impossible to believe there was ever a puppy born of any breed that wasn't absolutely adorable, at least until he was two months old! But if it is a JACK RUSSELL puppy—it is twice as adorable! One cannot choose a puppy on this basis alone. There are several aspects to taking on a responsibility that could last as long as sixteen years. It is all right to buy from a friend, or a friend of a friend, whose bitch just had a darling litter—but here are some things to consider.

No matter for what purpose your puppy is intended, you want a healthy, cheerful puppy—free of inherited faults and unsoundness and one who is a credit to the breed. Don't start out with a puppy, just because "he picked ME out"; or "isn't that crooked nose cute" etc. Later on you might find yourself making excuses for his shortcomings.

So where do you begin? Begin with a reputable breeder, small or large, who comes with a good reputation, either from others who have dealt with him, or the J.R.T.C.A. Do not hesitate to ask for one or two people to contact, who could give the breeder a reference.

Above all, do not buy from dealers (e.g. pet stores). You will have no guarantee of the puppy's origin, how far he has traveled while crated with other dogs who could be carrying a variety of diseases, or if the pedigree you are given is in any way correct, or how healthy he is and what immunization he has had.

There are two ways to buy puppies—one is to visit the kennel, meet the breeder, the parents of the puppies and any relations they might have on hand, and finally the puppies themselves. Tell the breeder what you want to do with the puppy and have enough confidence in him to let him lead you to the one that he thinks would suit your purpose. Remember, it is in his best interests, as well as yours, to make sure the puppy is a resounding success. There is no better advertisement for his kennel than a happy, satisifed owner. If you are interested in breeding, be guided by his choice—very often the "darling" of the litter is not the one that will win in conformation or go-to-ground classes later on. For instance, if you want to work your dog, he might show you a litter out of "the best working bitch I've ever owned" etc. Perhaps you just want a pet to romp with the children, or to go for walks in the woods with you. In this case he will probably show you the puppy in the litter who is not the most aggressive or super active. All puppies should be active, but hyper-activity could be the sign of nervousness, etc. If there is one in the litter who constantly hangs back and doesn't join in—ask about him. I have found, more than once, that this is the "thinker" in the crowd and the one who works everything out before leaping in—but maybe he is shy and a possible future problem, definitely unsuitable as a family pet or breeding stock. If you are unfamiliar with the breed, tell that to your seller. Put your trust in him and you'll come out on top.

The other method of buying is "over-the-phone." In this case, all the responsibility lies with the breeder and it is a big one. I have sent dogs all over the continent with gratifying success, but the responsibility always weighs heavily on me. I spend a great deal of time talking to my prospective buyer, in order to get a feeling of his personality and temperament, what he expects from his dogs, etc. Occasionally, I have eased out of selling someone a puppy, because I didn't feel they were suitable Jack Russell Terrier owners. Don't be "put-off" if you feel the breeder is interviewing you but take it the way it is intended; that he really cares about *his* dogs and what happens to them, and that is more important to him than making a sale. If the puppy is intended for use in a breeding program, I try to find out the type of dog(s) the buyer has already and then stick to his type—size, coat, etc., e.g., a puppy that will finish out at 14 inches would not be a good cross with a 10" dog—the produce would be far from uniform. If you want a rough coated litter you must breed rough to rough, as the rough coat is recessive and the smooth coat dominant. When you breed rough to smooth, you will probably get one or two rough coats and the rest will be smooth. Keeping the terrier's height down isn't too easy, as dogs are inclined to breed taller so if the terrier you want to breed is tall you should be looking for a slightly smaller dog for it's future mate.

Ready to take on the world at 6 months; a granddaughter of Hamilton breeding, owned by Brenda Cross.

At what age should you buy a puppy? It is generally agreed that a puppy should not be taken from his litter mates until he is at least six or seven weeks old. The next question is how old can he be, and still grow into a happy, well adjusted dog who is devoted to you and your family? Certainly anything younger than a year is still a puppy and is easily adopted into his new life style and family. You lose the fun and warmth of "cuddling" the puppy, but there are many advantages in getting an older one which might compensate. You know what he looks like, what kind of a coat he has, how his ears are set and what kind of a disposition he has. If he has grown up with his mother, she will have taught him the arts of hunting and going-to-ground. She will have taught him tug-of-war, when to run after his quarry, and when to be patient and wait for the right moment to make his move. It is marvelous to watch the older bitch, from six weeks on, gently encourage her child to pull and shake, and how she only will pull hard enough to make him work, but not so hard that he can't hang on and shake too! However, if the puppy is over four months old and has been strickly a kennel puppy, with little or no personal handling and human relationship, other than having feed pushed at him, I would think twice before making this purchase.

The following is a suggested list of questions you might ask your seller. Any reputable breeder would appreciate your interest and concern and would not hesitate to answer them to the best of his knowledge.

- When was he born?
- Has he been wormed (how many times) and has he had his DHLP-P shots?
- Has he had a rabies shot (*only* if over four months)?
- Is he a good eater?
- Does he have a good bite?—It should be a scissor bite, like a human's, with the top teeth overlapping and touching the bottom teeth; and the back teeth should meet exactly, top and bottom.
- Is his tail long enough?
- What are the temperaments of his mother and father?
- Is there any problem with fighting in the kennel?
- Is he a good car traveler?
- How much handling has he had, and has he been in the house, at all, with the family, etc.?
- Does he, in the opinion of the breeder, have good conformation according to the J.R.T.C.A. breed standard?
- Will his chest be small enough to be considered the right size for a Jack Russell Terrier?
- Have his parents been worked underground? (This is only important if you want to work him or use him in a breeding program).
- Do his parents show good sporting instincts?

If you do pick your puppy out in person, here is a suggested list of things to look out for—but the bottom line, in any case, *is whether the puppy appeals to you!* Young children, if along, need not take part in the final decision as they will love any puppy that goes home with them.

Faults To Look For

Red, brown or pink nose (cannot be registered). This refers to the part that has no hair, and not the skin and hair around it.

Blue eye(s)—they should be from auburn to dark brown.

Too much brown hair—if he has more than 50 percent brown hair, he cannot be registered as a Jack Russell.

Incorrect bite (see description under "Things to Ask")

Too long a back and too shallow a body (as seen from the side) which gives the appearance of a weasel body. This is not only very unattractive, but also it is very difficult to keep any weight on a dog built like this—and he will be lacking in stamina.

Legs too short

Chest too wide

Chest and rib cage round, *instead of* flat.

Bad feet—the feet should look like cat's feet and not like rabbit's feet; toes should be slightly arched, with good strong nails, both of which are needed for digging.

A good ear set—Most little puppies have a good ear set, so you will have to be guided by the parent's ears. They should fold forward and down, lie flat against the head and come just to the corner of the eye. If one or both of the parents' ears are not correct, I would worry about the puppy's ears finishing out correctly. *(N.B. Ears go a little crazy when the puppy is teething, but correct themselves in a few weeks).*

A shy puppy—Not to be confused with the thinker, the shy puppy will be noted if he continually ducks away from the breeder. He could be unsure of *you*—that would not necessarily mean he was shy—but if he is unsure of people who know and handle him, pick another puppy.

A constantly barking puppy—Leave him where you find him. He is probably nervous and lacking in confidence which is so important in a Jack Russell Terrier.

Long silky hair—The coat should be coarse and wiry if it is rough or broken, and not fine if it is smooth. It must be flat, whether he is rough, broken or smooth coated. If he is under two months it will be hard to tell about his final coat. The parents of the puppy will give you a better idea what to expect when he is mature.

Above all, the puppy should be alert, curious and outgoing. He should LOOK healthy, have clear eyes, no runny nose, pink gums, white teeth, a shiny coat with no signs of dandruff or red blotches on the skin. Be sure you get a current health certificate (within ten days of your picking him up) and a record of his worming and shots.

BASIL—3 months old. Owned by Winship Durrett.

Bringing Home Your Puppy

Buying a puppy is a traumatic experience not only for you and your family, but also for the puppy. Where do you start? We have dealt with how you choose your puppy, so we'll take it from there.

Timing is most important—true you can't tell the gods when to produce your puppy, but reliable breeders will keep him a reasonable length of time, until you are ready to take him home. Pick a date when you can spend time with him, when there are no visitors, parties, house-renovations (workers going in and out; cars and trucks on the move, etc.) and, last but not least, *not* at Christmas time. Nothing is more heartwarming than to see a smiling child holding a warm cuddly puppy on Christmas morning. But then what? There is no worse time to start out with a young puppy than over the Christmas holiday—too many visitors, too many people handling him, the outside doors opening and closing causing draughts and a chance of escape, tinsel to be chewed and swallowed, extra electric extensions so wonderful to chew, rich food indiscriminately handed out, and so on. If you want to give someone a Christmas puppy, have the breeder take one or two pictures, which can be put in a box and wrapped in Christmas paper and presented Christmas day. Delivery can then be taken when the household has returned to normal and is back on a regular routine—puppy included.

First of all—be prepared. Find out what the puppy has been eating and visit the grocery store. Fix a bed for him he can call his own. I prefer a closed-in kennel such as the airline type, which is available at most pet stores. As you will be using it for house-breaking, it shouldn't be so big that he can go to the bathroom at one end and still keep the other end clean. Your Jack Russell puppy is basically a clean animal, who will go to great lengths not to soil his sleeping quarters. Dogs in a wild state live in dens, but always go outside to defecate and urinate. Put a small piece of blanket or something soft that is easily washed, in the kennel with plenty of newspaper under it. In lieu of a kennel, you can get a large carton from your "friendly grocer," put a thin piece of plywood or masonite on the bottom and have a blanket or sheet across the top covering half of it, and you have a den. If you cover the whole carton, you must make two-inch holes around the top, so there will be plenty of ventilation. After a while, you will probably have to replace the carton. In the meantime, if there are children involved, they will have a marvelous time with it. I had one that I kept for years, because my artistic children had decorated it with windows, window boxes with flowers, a door frame, a sign above the door with the puppy's name on it, two chimneys, and ivy growing up the sides! This is your puppy's castle and his safe place—it is never to be used as a punishment, nor is he to be punished while he is in it. When you put him to bed at night, do so with a special edible treat.

You will need 3 bowls—one for his prepared food, one for his "free-choice" and one for his water. He will need plenty of chew toys. His first collar should be soft and come off easily. I like the cat collars (bell removed and without an elastic insert) as they come with a soft lining. Eventually he will need a proper leather collar (not plastic—they might be irritating) and leash. Your Jack Russell Terriers should never need a choke collar as they are easily restrained and trained. His lead training shouldn't start before he is 10-12 weeks old.

When you pick up your puppy, the seller will provide you with a health certificate (dated within 10 days of delivery), and a health record giving a history of worming, shots, and any sickness or injury he might have had, plus his breeding certificate and pedi-gree. Finally, if he is going home by car, find out if he has had car rides before and how he reacted. If he only has had car rides when he was taken to the veterinarian, I strongly recommend giving him the appropriate sleeping pill or an anti-emetic. Consult your vete-

Play (children and terriers) love to play to-gether.

ALWAYS WILLING TO TAKE A RIDE!

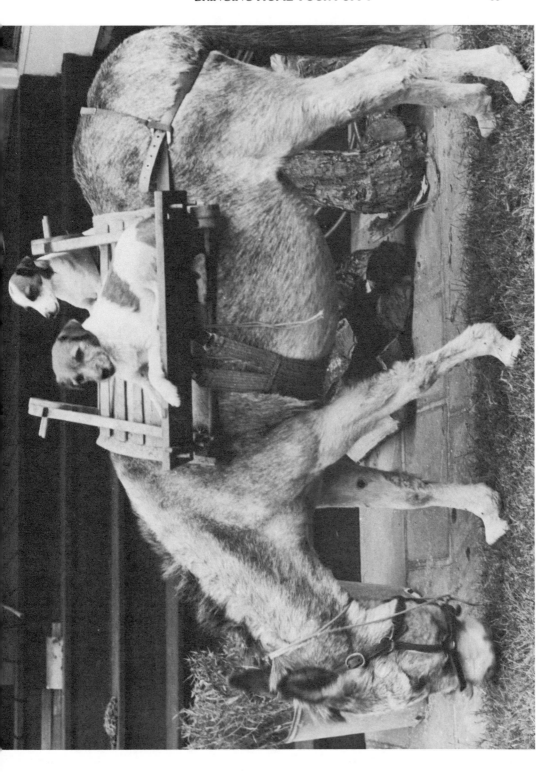

Sometimes this self-feeding is pretty hard work for us little guys!

rinarian about what and how much to give your puppy and get it from him. If your puppy becomes car-sick, on his first long car ride, it will be difficult (not impossible—see chapter on Travel) to get him over being car-sick during future car rides. Have someone hold him on their lap who will pat him and reassure him, the day you pick him up.

His castle, his den, his safe place.

So now he is home! For the next few weeks he should be confined in a small area, where you can keep an eye on him. Put him outside frequently. Go out with him and praise him when he performs his duty. It is no use just sticking him out the door—even if it's raining or cold. You must go outside with him yourself. Take him to the same spot each time, and it won't be long before he gets the idea that the sooner he performs, the sooner he can go back inside. After he has been home an hour or two, confine him to his new box or kennel and let him sleep. Puppies play hard and must sleep hard. If he has been in his new box a few times during the day, he will probably cry very little, if at all, his first night in his new home. Someone should volunteer to take him out once or twice during the night.

It is fine to allow people to pat and play with your puppy, but do not allow rough handling. The terrier puppy will give the impression he's enjoying it—but it isn't good for him, just the same.

Do not let people swoop over him with "Oh, isn't he dar-ling" and then pick him up. It will not be long before he will start shying away from *your* hand. When he is picked up, support his hindquarters with one hand and hold him under his chest with the other. *Never* pick him up by his front legs. From time to time, he may be picked up by the scruff of his neck, by taking hold of the loose skin at the back of his neck, and *without twisting it* lift him straight up. Don't clamp down on the skin any more than necessary. It is important to do this because, terrier-like, someday he will get in a situation where he will have to be hauled to safety by the scruff of his neck. If he's used to it, he will not struggle when someone grabs hold of him. Once in a while, for the same reason, I gently pull the puppy around by his tail. You can also stroke the underneath side of his tail. When you first start this, he will probably object, slam his tail down tightly between his legs and try to get away from your hand. Gently, but firmly, keep trying and eventually he will be relaxed and will actually enjoy it. Always stroke in the direction of the hair growth-never against. There is nothing more frustrating than trying to pull a terrier out of a hole, when every time he feels you touch his tail he jams it between his legs!

Treat your puppy, from the day he arrives at your home, the way he is to continue his life with you—from his sleeping quarters, to his daily routine, to his feeding spot, and to his restrictions. For instance, if he is not going to be allowed on the furniture, beds, etc., (with which I totally agree) start this from the beginning. *"NO"* is the word he must learn. Just say it firmly, using his name *first,* ("Static, NO") and then correct what he is doing wrong, I have found it almost unnecessary to spank my terriers. Even when older, scolding generally is enough.

House Breaking

There have been reams and reams written on the subject of "House Breaking" a puppy and/or adult dog and all of it worthwhile, if not exactly in total agreement. As far as the Jack Russell Terrier is concerned, if he is started correctly at 12-14 weeks, he is one of the easiest of all breeds to train. His intelligence, his eagerness to please, plus his natural instinct to be clean, makes the training short and simple, with the one provision—we repeat—if it is carried on correctly and routinely.

Recently a short Bantam Book has been published on this subject alone that is *excellent,* and could not be improved on for the Jack Russell Terrier. So, rather than devoting a chapter of this book to housebreaking your terrier puppy I recommend this 67 page, easy to follow, book as being an excellent system:

"How to House Break Your Dog in Seven Days." by Shirley Kalstone, published by Bantam Books.

However, I will add a few suggestions. Before you start your house training, be sure your puppy is in good health, (no worms, no sniffling nose, no dull, dry, coat, etc.) is happy and relaxed in his new home, and has a den, crate, or something similar, where he can be contained in a small, supervised area that he knows well and where he is comfortable and settled. Miss Kalstone is explicit on the different types of arrangements that are ideal.

The Jack Russell Terrier is a go-to-ground dog, and does love "a roof over his head"! If you use a pen (rather than a crate) take a corner and cover it with a piece of cardboard, masonite, or a blanket, where he can go and feel as if he were tucked away in his "den" as he would do in the wild. Also, for the short time he is being trained, the fewer dogs milling around the better. Keep the confusion in the household to a minimum—it is definitely *not* the time to re-do the kitchen, for instance!

The Schedule

The success of house breaking is dependent on how meticulous you are about keeping to a schedule—Miss Kalstone makes this very clear. Even after your puppy is housetrained, he will be more likely to stay trained if he is on a regular routine. Here is a suggested program which includes his feeding times (it follows one of Miss Kalstone's schedules). Obviously, the hours can be changed a little, to suit your sleeping hours, but the time span remains the same. Be sure your puppy is confined to his crate or corner with chew toys and/or bones, when you are away from home, asleep, or anytime you are too busy to keep an eye on him. This way bad habits never get started. After he is house-broken, when he is confined he can have free choice puppy chow as well as a bowl of clean water. (*The confining to his crate, most of the time is just until he is trained which lasts seven days, AT THE MOST.)*

7:00 a.m.—Wake up—take puppy out *immediately* (not after you shower, etc.)

7:10-7:30 a.m.—Free period with you, while you dress and make breakfast at the same time keeping a watch on him.

7:30 a.m.—Breakfast—puppy chow, mixed and softened with warm water and mixed with a little *high* quality canned dog food; or fatless table scraps—you can add a teaspoon of bacon fat, but no other fat.

8:00 a.m.—Another period outside.

8:15-8:45 a.m.—Inside for unconfined time with you and then confined in his kennel or den.

8:45 a.m.—Confined. After he is housetrained, he can stay free until noon—provided you can watch him—or he can be outside if you have a closed-in yard or live in the country.

12:00 Noon—Feed: a small meal (milk and bread, or some cottage cheese, or cooked egg, etc.)

12:30 p.m.—Outside with you.

12:30-5:00 p.m.—Repeat the 8:45 to noon routine.

5:00 p.m.—Supper—same as breakfast—this should be his last food until 7:30 a.m.

5:30 p.m. Outside with you.

5:45-8:30 p.m.—Repeat 8:45 to noon routine.

8:30 p.m.—Outside with you.

8:45-11:00 p.m.—Inside with you.

11:00 p.m.—Outside with you, then in his kennel for the night. If he is housetrained, leave him with a small amount of water and give him one or two dog biscuits as a treat. If he is not housetrained, no water and only one biscuit.

Remember—praise is the key to success, and no physical punishment—only scolding is enough. When he is confined to his kennel he should have chew toys and maybe a marrowbone or some form of entertainment.

(Editor's Note: This schedule is for a young, not fully trained, puppy, which may be modified as the puppy matures and becomes fully housetrained. If you work all day, modify it to meet your away-from-home hours, leaving the puppy crated, with chew toys etc.—no food and only a little water, until he is going all day

without mistakes, which will probably only be a few days—and then he can be left with free choice food, and, water. I repeat, this schedule is ONLY FOR HOUSE TRAINING which should not last more than SEVEN DAYS.)

Keep your puppy clean all the time, especially his "private parts," even if this means washing that area. Dogs, unlike cats, do not bathe themselves. They will lick mud, etc. off their paws, but that's about it. If a puppy doesn't smell clean, his desire to be clean is obviously lessened. The same applies to his crate or kennel. If he does make a mistake in it, wash the blanket, thoroughly wash the crate, spray it with a disinfectant, and line it with fresh newspapers. The cleaner and sweeter it smells, the more likely the puppy will want to keep it that way. A few years ago, we were having little success in training one of our dogs. Two or three nights a week he would defecate in his kennel, and we would wash the blanket and change the papers, but still he made the odd mistake. One day, I decided to "spring-clean" his kennel, and when I lifted up the board covering the bottom, I was horrified. Apparently, he had been urinating during the night, but by the morning the papers had dried so we thought he was only doing the one thing! I cleaned the dickens out of the kennel—and we tried again. From then on, we had no more "morning messages"!

If you have a female puppy, and she urinates a little, when she is excited—do not scold her, but don't pick her up. Just ignore her for a minute or two, and then pat her. She has no control over the "dribbling" and would have no idea what she was doing wrong. This is a puppy trait, which is soon outgrown. By the same token if the female puppy squirms up to you on her tummy don't pat her, pick her up or look at her! She'll soon learn if she wants attention, to stay on her feet.

If you are housetraining two or more puppies at the same time, add different food color to their food, and then you can tell which puppy made the mistake. Take him over to it, scold him (do not hit him) and put him outside with more cross words.

Your Jack Russell Terrier is very gregarious and loves to be with people. The more you keep him with you, the better he will be. He will develop more personality if as a young puppy, he can spend as much of his awake hours with you as possible. Don't be afraid to take him around with you. If he has been properly immunized, there is very little chance of his "catching something." His exposure to different situations, people, noise, etc., will make him socially better, and later on a superior workng hunter as he will not be upset by new demands and problems.

The most important thing is to ENJOY your puppy and be relaxed about his training. You will find him the most adaptable dog of any breed I know. He will join in, with enthusiasm, any sport, game, hunt or "happening." The anecdotes in this book verify that.

Your puppy (dog) must be weighed to determine the amount of worming medi-cine, or any other medication, he should be given.

Basic Training and Good Manners for your Jack Russell Terrier

The better behaved and more socially balanced your dog becomes, the more popular you both will be! He will be only as well mannered as you expect him to be. The Jack Russell Terrier is a loving, anxious-to-please animal, who will always try to do what you want. The bottom line is to *know* what you want and not to change your mind. Don't ask him to do something he can't possibly understand, and then throw up your hands and say "Oh, he's hopeless." Poor fellow—he does not speak English, Russian, or any other language, and can only learn through persistent, patient training. If you are unsure of yourself as a basic teacher, seek help from someone who is successful in this line. If you take him to a training school, make sure the trainer is not the kind that teaches through rough and unsympathetic handling, but one who "accentuates the positive"! Do not overtrain your terrier—a terrier must be independent, a thinker, one who can make a quick decision if need be. An over-disciplined terrier is likely to lose his integrity or even worse, his self-confidence. As an owner/breeder of Jack Russell Terriers says, "You don't discipline your terrier, you have successful negotiations with him."

He needs to know how to come when called; how to lead (on your left side) *without pulling;* wait at a door when it is opened and not bolt through it; stay in a car when the door is opened, or when the windows are left open; not to jump on the furniture; not to jump up on people (this is the hardest of all and must be started from the first day in your home); to stop playing and be quiet in the house when asked; if indicated, not run sheep, horses, cattle, cars, bicycles, etc., and to mind his manners at all times.

Starting at square one—teach him his name right away. I recommend a two syllable name—such as "my book" terrier—"Static." That way he has a double chance at hearing his name—say it like this: "STA-tic." It is very easy for your puppy to learn his name. Have *small* tidbits handy when you say his name, and give him one. Keep the morsels tiny (dog biscuits, dog candy, pieces of meat, etc.) He won't know the difference in size and you don't want to spoil his taste for his regular, rather dull (by comparison) meals. It won't be long before his name means something interesting. Make sure you say his name clearly and say it over and over while you reward him.

At this point I want to stress the importance of being able to take food away from your puppy. This is a matter of safety, not only for him, but for anyone else such as a small child who might approach the puppy while he is eating and perhaps get his face bitten. From the dog's side of it, there will be a time when he is eating something injurious or fatal to himself. I am reminded of the time a dog, belonging to a friend of mine, got hold of her diet pills and ate the whole bottle because she couldn't take it from him. It was too late by the time she got him to the veterinarian. Had she trained the dog since he was a puppy to allow her to take whatever was in his mouth from him this story would have quite a different ending. So, once in a while take away a bone, a tidbit, etc., from your puppy, praise him and then give it right back to him. Someday you'll be glad you did this.

When you have two or more dogs it is good training, and very easy, to feed them a "treat" only when you call *his* name. They will all sit around you waiting for their name to be called. If they grab someone else's treat, quickly say (for example) "Static, NO," and take it from him (One use of the lesson talked about in the preceeding paragraph).

Teach him to come by saying his name and the words "come here." e.g.—"STA-tic, come here." He will probably run about more or less ignoring you. Keep saying his name and "come here"—keep your eyes fixed on him as you follow him around

This terrier bitch, WALNUT, owned by Ontario, Canada breeder, Lynn Westaway, jumps on the sheep for a free ride nearly everyday! The sheep don't mind her at all, in fact they seem to enjoy her company.

HERITAGE JANE RUSSELL and her puppies—owned by Victor Heerman, Lexington, Kentucky. by Christine Picavet, 1984.

slowly. When he does come, praise him and give him a tidbit. Don't ask him to come to you, if you're in a situation where you can't win—e.g. outside where you can't possibly get at him, or when he's running game, etc. Never punish him when he does come to you. Yelling is a "no, no"—it only makes him nervous and insecure, and he'll get worse instead of better.

Teaching the puppy to lead is a simple task which should be taught as soon as possible after he is ten to twelve weeks old. Before you start the leading lessons, have him wear his collar (a softly lined cat collar, without elastic is the best at this age) for a few days, until he has forgotten all about it. For the first session, attach a leash to the collar, and while you hold on to it, follow him around. When he becomes used to the fact that you are part of him, gently pull him towards you, offering him a delectable morsel. He will probably panic, throw himself down, roll over, etc. Keep talking to him and reassure him all is well. When he does come in the direction of the pull—a few steps are enough—praise him and give him the tidbit. Repeat this, until he reacts to the pull without hesitation. Fifteen minutes is enough for the first lesson which can be repeated later on the same day. Encourage him to come with you, following that thing that seems to be attached to him, by enticing him with some good smelling meat and patting your left leg. In a few lessons he will be leading without restraint. By the third or fourth lesson he can be taught to lead correctly. This means he always walks on your left side, with his ribcage by your left leg, without pulling forward, or dragging behind. Don't let him hang on his collar. The technique is simple—one short sharp jerk, then a quick release by immediately thrusting your left hand forward. The left hand holds the leash, and the end of the leash is held loosely in your right hand. Always make the lead-work a joyous occasion. Give him small treats and keep telling him "what fun we're having!" This will pay off if you show him in conformation classes. He will trot gaily along beside you, proudly carrying his head and tail.

When he is six months or older you can teach him not to bolt through the outside door when you open it. At no time, before or after this training, do you touch him with your foot. You can put it out as a signal not to pass you—but if you take a swipe at him with it, all you will do is scare him and make him try to go past you faster, in order to out do you. The first step is to open the door just wide enough so your body fills the gap and, putting up your hand say

"Static, stay (or wait)." Keep saying it and pat him! Open the door wider, and repeat the words—again praising him. Then close the door, and stay inside with him, telling him what a fine fellow he is. Practice this several times and then call it a day. Do this for a few days. The next step is to start as in step number one, but after a few seconds, go outside, leaving him inside. Wait a few minutes and then come back. When you can do this, while your puppy remains calm and makes no effort to go out, you are ready for step number three. Repeat step number one, wait a few minutes and then say in a low voice "All right Static, you may go out now" and let him march out quietly beside you. I have found this training to be very useful in so many situations—around the house, traveling (motels, elevators, and such), shopping, getting in and out of cars, and later on, when he is being trained to go to ground.

The same applies to the car. He must be taught not to jump out of it when you open the door. I have a rolled newspaper, magazine or some such soft thing ready. I open the door and say "Static, stay." If he makes a leap, bop him gently on the nose, or on top of his head and say "Static-*NO*!" If he got out, go and get him, put him in the car, and try again. It helps if he is wearing his collar and long leash as you can easily catch him if he does get loose. Also, if he is attached to a leash, you can grab it as he shoots past you, give it a good jerk, and say "STATIC, NO." Immediately put him back in the car uttering cross words as you do. Eventually, you'll be able to load the groceries, shopping, etc. and probably he'll sleep through the whole operation. As far as teaching him not to jump out open car windows, leave them down, go a few feet behind the car, and watch. When he goes to jump out say "Static, NO" and throw a soft object at him. This needs to be repeated only once or twice and he'll get the idea. Needless to say when you are away from the car, the windows shouldn't be down so far that the dog can jump out.

Teaching your puppy not to jump up on people starts from the day you bring him home. Refrain from picking him up (hard to do!) and ask others not to pick him up as well. Talk to him at his height level, e.g. sit on a stool, squat down, etc. It is too early to scold him—you don't want to discourage his puppy love and enthusiasm, so you just use repetition and practice at this point. *Never* hit him on the head. It will only make him shy of your hand and you. I have never had any luck stepping on hindfeet, as a lot of trainers recommend. I guess the terrier's feet are too small! I have resorted to a tap on the nose—but that should be rare. When he's older, if he jumps up on a visitor, say "Static, DOWN," give him a good spank on his bottom, and ask your visitor not to pat him. If the friend smiles sweetly and says "Oh, that's all right. I like dogs." or "he can smell my dogs!" etc., explain that you are teaching him not to jump up and that it would help you if he would just sit down and ignore the dog for the time being. When the excitement of a new person is over, he can pat and talk to him, *quietly.* Another method is to bend your knee quickly and bump him in his chest (if he's tall enough) saying "Static, DOWN."

Barbara Woodhouse has an excellent method of breaking an older dog from jumping up. It takes two people—yourself and a helper. You leave the house for awhile, so your dog will be over-joyed when you come home. He is held on a long line, attached to the collar, by your helper. As you approach him (the line being loose at this point) he will jump up. As soon as he does, put your hand out in a flat position and say "Static, DOWN" while at the same time, the helper pulls him down with the line. Repeat this, each time he jumps up. Praise him extravagantly when he doesn't jump up. Do this for two or three days in a row, and he will probably be broken from this annoying habit. This method is only applicable to a dog over six months old. If you have discouraged your puppy from jumping up from the time he was little, probably this lesson will not be necessary.

Breaking your puppy from running horses, cattle, etc. is a lot more difficult and should not be attempted until he is no longer a puppy, with puppy ways, and is obedient to coming when called. The very first time he does chase something that is not allowed is the time to really punish him. Saying "Static, NO," you get your hands on him as soon as possible (*N.B. do not call him to you—you must go to him*) and give him a pretty good whaling with the flat of your hand on his backside, while you let him hang as you hold him by the scruff of his neck. Again *never* yell, and don't let anyone else but you call to him. When sheep are in the picture, every training step must be taken. The first day, walk him on a long lead—letting him range ahead. Walk through the sheep. If he makes a move to charge them, give him a good jerk saying "Static, NO." Do this a few times. If he continues to try to chase them, then give him a couple of good licks with the end of the lead. Repeat this until he is really steady. Then he is ready to walk off the line through the sheep. Eventually he will be completely sheep trained and you can be relaxed about walking or riding through, or past, a flock. We ride past our neighbours' sheep with 8-10 terriers and not one will chase them, even when the sheep start running.

Chasing cars, bicycles, and motorcycles must be and can be easily cured. If he is not cured, it is only a matter of time before your dog will make that one final mistake. Get a friend to drive their car where the chase usually takes place. You hide in the car and when the chase is on, throw a bucket of water on him, or shoot him with a water pistol! The same works with the bikes—only it will have to be a water pistol—it would be a little difficult carrying and dumping a pail of water while riding a two-wheeler!

As far as fighting or snapping at anyone, (postman included), it is not to be allowed from the time you get your puppy. When he's small, it might be considered "funny," but as he matures, so will his growl and bite.

The Jack Russell Terrier does have to be brave enough to stand up to a fox, coon, groundhog, badger, etc. which takes a lot of courage and agility. He must make some kind of racket, in order for the terrier man to know where to dig. It is basically foolhardy, and sometimes suicidal, to actually pick a fight underground. He must be strong enough to defend himself, if caught in the open with his adversary, but why should this mean he has to snarl and snap at people? It doesn't, nor should it be tolerated. The terrier is a very intelligent, discriminating dog. He can be taught when and where to mind his manners, just as a well trained attack dog can be an "old shoe" when not on duty. One day an Englishman, who was reputed as a terrier authority, picked up my male, Hard Sauce, and after giving him a good shake remarked, "He should have at least shown his teeth." I replied, "He would have had his socks knocked off him if he had!" This dog has a marvelous disposition and, as a result, I can take him anywhere—and I do! I do not allow any fighting amongst my terriers at home or at a trials, yet when they are out working their game (quarry), they are ferocious, fearless and have accounted for many tough animals. The "snappy" reputation that sometimes follows the Jack Russell Terrier is not necessary or fair. Owners should and can expect the same good manners from their terriers they expect from other people's children!

I remember standing beside a terrier ring, watching a dog puppy class (six months to a year) and one puppy kept turning around, growling and snapping at the puppy behind him. The lady showing the puppy who was being snapped at, kept backing up, politely trying to get away from the brat. However, the holder of the "showing-off" puppy thought it was terribly amusing and did nothing to stop him. I was appalled, and finally, when the lady turned an imploring look at me, I could take it no longer and asked the other handler to remonstrate with his puppy, explaining he was scaring the lady's puppy. I won't describe the look I got! However, he did move the puppy up and away from the other fellow with heartfelts thanks coming my way from the distraught lady. Someday, that show-off will turn into a little horror, liked only by his owners and, at the same time giving the Jack Russell Terrier a bad name.

Whatever you are asking your terrier to do at the moment must be completed even if it takes a long patient hour! Also, if you have decided that he is not to be allowed to do something, like jump on your brocade couch, it is most important not to change your mind with, "Oh well, he can do it, just this time." Unlike children you can't explain why he can do something today, and not tomorrow. There are no grey areas with a dog—it is either "Yes" or "No."

Continual yapping is absolutely unnecessary. It is alright to let "Static" sound the alarm, with a couple of barks, but not to yap on and on. He must be silenced and usually "Static, be qui-ET" is enough. However, if it takes something more, do it until he does stop. Don't give up with, "I can't shut him up!" Stick with it! Even banging on the window probably will stop him (I know, someday, I'm going to over-do it and break the glass, as a friend of mine once did!). You can even resort to throwing a shoe out the window at him! (Don't forget to pick it up, before Static does!)

Like small children, your puppy can only learn one lesson at a time. Take them in order and be firm but patient. Training and maturing into an obedient well adjusted dog is built on "Uncompromising Kindness."

Obedience training following the A.K.C. requirements is, in my opinion, unkind to dogs and most especially to an enthusiastic, self-motivated terrier. To ask him to sit motionless in a spot where he probably would never choose to sit, while his handler marches around and around him, looking like a graven image, cannot possibly be anything but awful for him. It doesn't prove anything except that he can sit still for ages, feeling miserable—and for what purpose? Don't use your terrier to entertain you or boost your own ego. He is a fun-loving, marvelous character who wants to love you, have fun with you, and go hunting with you.

When puppies are teething, their ears often go "crazy" for a few weeks.

The "Non-Eater"

"I have tried everything and he won't eat anything but raw hamburger"—I have heard this more than once. If your dog has become spoiled to the point where he is not eating properly—here's a program to follow.

The "not-eating" has become a habit, and "Static" is probably refusing to eat anything but the tastiest food, which doesn't make a nutritious and well balanced diet. Changing the feeding pattern of a dog in this frame of mind, is going to take a certain amount of will power and determination on your part. Don't worry, he won't let himself starve to death. Make up your mind that it might take 3-4 days before he gets hungry enough to eat. If he has a kennel he sleeps in give him his offered meals where he can eat undisturbed. Allow him 5-10 minutes eating time—after that, if he hasn't finished it all, pick up the uneaten food—*throw it out* and try again the next meal. His bowls, including his water bowl should be kept clean, meaning washed in hot water and soap. You are probably proud of the wonderful nose (the ability to smell rabbit tracks, etc.) your dog has. This wonderful nose can also smell old food, stale water, etc. much better than you possibly can—yet you would not think of eating your dinner off your unwashed lunch plate or drink your wine out of last night's unwashed wine glass!

Offer him *very* small amounts at first (a tablespoon or so—no more. The first time he does finish up, praise him—but don't offer anymore. As he gets the eating habit, increase the amounts slowly—you'll get along better if he's hungry. NO TABLE FOOD or tasty additions, at this point. Later on, you can save your good scraps and mix them with his food. But *never* feed him anything from the table. It will take him awhile (maybe as long as a month) to get over the shock, but stick to it. It's worth it. *Feed at the same time* everyday. He should eat twice a day at least up to eight months, at which time he is old enough to be fed just once a day. After he's eating his offered meals, you can leave dry food out for him all day, as well (called free-choice.)

Dogs, young and old, should have access to fresh water at all times. It should be changed at least twice a day.

Self-feeding!

Marrow bones are excellent chew toys and they last for days.

Who threw this away up here, anyway?

At 3 months, WOODLUCK ZABAGLIONE is ready for the game!

Free Choice Feeding for the Mature Dog

There are many adult dogs, who do not have regular meals, but live on a "free choice" feeding program. This means they can eat whenever they want—as they would if they were in a wild state. The dry food is left in a large pan, with *fresh* water beside it. This is all the feed my mature dogs get—not counting treats (usually dog biscuits) and marrow bones, knuckles or any HARD bone that won't splinter. *Never* fowl or lamb bones as they splinter badly. Our terriers work hard, probably covering 15 miles a day, following the horses when we ride. Three or four sets of horses go out of our stable each day—and it is only "by the hardest," that the terriers can be kept from joining in. If we ride five miles, they probably go ten—considering the hunting, searching the woods and checking every hole, they do! They are all hard as nails, carry good flesh, but are *not* overweight and often go to ground after foxes, ground-hogs, etc. in some very tight places!

Even if your dog does not take a lot of exercise each day, he will probably eat only the amount of free choice he needs. The first few days he will gorge himself, if this is a new system for him, but he'll soon taper off his intake. However, if he does become too fat and stays that way, then it is not a suitable programme for him. Conversely, if he doesn't hold his weight (assuming he is healthy and has been checked for worms) it isn't suitable either—but maybe another brand of dry food would work well for him.

There are many excellent free choice foods, Purina Dog Chow probably being the most widely used. Whatever you decide to feed your dog, unless you are knowledgeable on nutrition for dogs, check with your veterinarian to make sure the brand you are feeding contains everything your dog needs, for a balanced healthful diet.

airplane travel is easy for dogs to-day.

Initial Training to Go-To-Ground

Consider that going-to-ground is the terrier's most basic instinct (terra-ground) other than eating and breeding. The Jack Russell Terrier is king in this department, so "teaching" him to go-to-ground is hardly the correct word. "Encourage" is more like it. Personally, I have never had the experience of training a Jack Russell to do this, because all my dogs have gone to ground on their own, having been taught by the older dogs. However, if you own a single Jack Russell terrier and you have had him from the time he was a pup, you might have to train him to "go-to-ground." I would not advise starting this until he is at least eight to ten months old. When you do start working with him it must be done with care and thought, *as a scare at this age might have a lasting effect.*

If there isn't a "canine teacher" available, build a tunnel out of three wooden planks, each about 10 feet long. The three planks are nailed to-gether at right angles to each other, making a 3 sided square, which becomes a tunnel when put on the ground (the ground makes the fourth side). Throw some raw meat in it, and your young terrier will scramble after it. Two or three throws and he'll run right through! Then find a place where you can put this tunnel partly under the ground and again put a treat at the end of it.

Once he has done this a few times he will go-to-ground any chance he can get. If he finds a quarry, encourage him to bark and/or make a racket so that you can hear him from on top. Again praise and encourage him. You now have a go-to-ground terrier and your fun with him is just beginning.

(See next chapter for further training.)

"They seldom die in bed, but most often with their boots on."

"Although we have had many dogs, Leo is the most honest, trust-worthy REAL dog we've had. As a hunter he is unbeatable, and as a companion he is faithful and true. He is also stubborn, self-willed and has a very powerful personality."

Working Jack Russell Terriers

John and Barbara Lowery

Jack Russell Terriers in the Eastern and Southern United States of America have an abundance of quarry on which to test their working skills. The most abundant and pesty is the woodchuck or groundhog, who is a sporting marmot and is considered vermin. Because they ruin acres of soybeans and pasture land, they are abhorred by farmers. Their earths are the size of British rabbit warrens, and it is generally agreed that a terrier with a chest that measures 16 inches at the largest part (right behind the elbows) is the maximum size that allows a terrier to get up to them. (The length of leg has little to do with it, but they should be long enough to go beyond the terrier's muzzle—as this helps protect his face against his underground adversary.) A larger terrier is useful at the end of the dig, which will be explained later.

Groundhogs are hibernators, so the best hunting is from about the first of May until the first of November. As the soil warms up in the early spring, the groundhogs wake up and can be seen sunning themselves close to their earths. Hunting is sporadic in the spring, the serious hunting starting in early June.

A maximum of four terriers hunting at one time are all that are needed. It should be remembered that the confines of an earth are very small, and one terrier working up to the quarry is usually

sufficient. Putting a very keen terrier in behind the terrier who is
barking at the quarry may cause the up-front terrier to receive
needless injuries, because he is interfering with the ability of the
front terrier to dodge and jump back. A typical team of four terriers
consists of two very small dogs, usually bitches, a medium sized
dog and a larger draw dog or "hole-ender." The small bitches are
allowed to run free, if it is a safe area, to check the earths for scent.
The other terriers are kept on couples and leashes until the quarry
is located. The little bitches hunt by going into an earth to search
the tunnels, or by merely poking their heads into it and giving a
snort. If the groundhog is home they will know, and one of them
will immediately go to ground. Depending on the size of it she may
find quickly, but she might have to explore for a time to get up to
the groundhog. This locating stage of the hunt is complicated by
the fact that groundhogs may push dirt behind them, in front of the
terrier, which is called "the throwback," or "dig away" if they feel
threatened. In this situation the value of an experienced terrier
cannot be overstated, as she will know to lie in the tunnel and bay
(bark) at the "throwback." How far the ground hog can dig on
seems to vary with soil type, but by knowing the terrier, the soil and
the terrain, you can still have in a successful hunt.

*The younger bitch (left) is gaining confidence by having with her an older and more
experienced bitch (right) while baying at the ground-hog. It should be emphasized it is
usually unwise to put two terriers at the same time into an earth which has not been
opened up. The rear terrier interferes with the ability of the front terrier to nip and dodge,
which might cause her to receive unnecessary bites. Also one terrier, by working in an
earth where the ground-hog has dug itself, dissipates the ground-hog's scent and the
presence of a second terrier will only make a difficult job harder by adding more scent. In
this photo the trench is sufficiently large for both terriers to work together in safety. John
and Barbara Lowery's FLIRT and QUICK working in Alabama.*

When the hole dog does "find," she will bay furiously and drive the groundhog to a block end and pin him there. As he may try to bolt if pressured, all the other openings should be stopped. A groundhog is such an efficient digger he may dig up through the ground and bolt through a new hole. We have known them to dig up under our feet, or under the noses of terriers waiting their turn outside the hole! Avoid the temptation to enter another terrier at this point, as it will only confuse the terrier working closest to the quarry and may cause her to receive unnecessary bites.

Once the groundhog is pinned down it is time to start the dig. We use an electronic locator collar to locate the terrier. We consider this collar to be essential for anyone working terriers in the earth. A frequent mistake of the novice is to try to determine where the baying is by how it sounds at the entrance. The earth is amazingly insulating and deceiving. It may be possible to locate the position of the terrier by listening from on top of the tunnel, but the electronic collar is much more reliable and a very small investment compared to the time it saves, as well as the safety it affords. Once the terrier is located, a hole or trench is dug down to the barking terrier, with care being taken during the last foot or so from the terrier as the hole might collapse behind the terrier, which could be fatal. The small terrier is removed and put on couples staked several feet from the entrance. She has done her job. A word of advice and caution is in order at this point. It is useless to let the small terrier keep hammering at the groundhog. She will only get bitten about the face and head and will not be able to draw (out) the varmint anyway. A small terrier badly mauled by a groundhog could be out of action for two weeks, so leave the rough stuff to the "hole-ender," or simply dig out the groundhog, catch him by the tail, and do whatever you wish with him.

The earth can now be opened up and cleaned out and a course of action chosen. It is important not to tarry at this point, as without a terrier in the ground to worry it, the quarry will turn and dig away, possibly necessitating an additional trench. Now may be the time for a larger, harder draw dog or the "hole-ender" mentioned earlier. If the groundhog is to be moved, rather than killed, because he is destroying crops or pasture land, take the groundhog from his earth by entering the "hole-ender" in the earth and he will draw the ground hog out of his hole. This saves extra digging as he will be a short distance from where you took out the smaller dog. Quickly grab the groundhog by the tail, choke the terrier off the groundhog and put him in a box, or burlap sack, for his removal to another place. Don't worry about the hole-ender doing him any serious harm, as it would be a rare occasion that a terrier could single-handedly kill a groundhog below ground.

After the hunt, check your terriers for injuries. Very few bites are serious, but still need to be cleaned and antibiotic ointment applied. Bites of the eyelid may require a stitch or two. Another health precaution is to be aware of the possibility of heat stroke. The best groundhog hunting is in the hot part of the summer, so a very excited, keen terrier may work past his limit. If you notice a terrier who is wobbly or panting much harder than usual, drop him into cool water. If the dog does not come right quickly, take him to a veterinarian immediately. In the hot weather hunting just after dawn will help avoid this problem. *(See chapter on Travel.)*

In consideration of the landowner, replace dirt which has been piled outside the hole during the dig. Having to drive his tractor over a pile of dirt may make the farmer consider the hunter more of a nuisance than the groundhogs! Loose dirt is easy to move, and the few minutes it takes will be well worth the trouble to insure future invitations to hunt.

Raccoon and possum also provide a challenge for the Eastern and Southern terrier. The raccoon is a tree dweller who is only occasionally found underground. Your best bet to find the raccoon is to hunt rock holes in the winter or make friends with some coonhunters and hunt with them, using your terriers when their hounds put a 'coon to ground rather than up a tree. The raccoon can inflict severe damage to a terrier and should be hunted only by experienced terriers and terrier persons.

It is possible to have some foxhunting with terriers in the South. Most of our work on foxes is by hunting rock holes in severe winter weather as the fox only goes to ground in the South when the weather is cold or to have its cubs. Southern foxes (unlike their slightly larger, unrelated Northern counterpart) are mostly small (8-10 pounds) so it will take a small chested terrier to get up to him. Most organized foxhunts do not dig out foxes when they go to ground, so your chance to do the real thing, e.g. bolt a fox for waiting hounds, will be limited. I am whipper-in to the Mooreland Hunt and in some areas I am asked to carry a small bitch in a bag for bolting fox. Although supportive of terrier work, our Master Harry Rhett, M.F.H. will almost always leave a fox for another day if he goes to ground. For this work I always use a small, very soft-type barking terrier, never one that has a tendency to close hard on her quarry.

Although the Jack Russell Terrier is primarily an earth worker, he is very adapt at squirrel hunting and is used often for this purpose. A good squirrel dog will trail a squirrel up a tree by scent and bark to summon the hunter to the spot. In some parts of the country a good squirrel dog is worth his weight in gold, and most Jack Russell Terriers take to it with great enthusiasm!

It is obvious there are different types of terrier work and a particular terrier may be better suited for one type than another. Although the Jack Russell Terrier was originally bred to hunt English fox and badger, they do *very* well in this country as their work style, which is to bark, worry, and nip, at its quarry, is very effective on fox, raccoon, groundhog and opossum.

A word of advice is in order on working your terriers in an earth. *There is potential danger every time a terrier goes to ground so it should not be taken lightly.* Until you are skilled and knowledgeable in this activity, learn how to work your terriers by hunting with someone who is experienced and has experienced terriers. Most people who work terriers underground will be more than happy to have you hunt with them and share their talents and knowledge with you. There is no need for unnecessary worry about working your terrier in an earth. If it is done properly there is little danger of losing him. What risk there is, will be well worth allowing your terrier to do what his ancestors were bred to do for many, many generations. Most people find, once they start hunting their Jack Russell Terriers, that something very special develops between terrier and person that can only come from allowing or encouraging your dog to do something it truly loves.

The favorite person of any breed of dog, whether it is a hound, bird dog, sheep dog or terrier, is the one who shows him sport. He even comes ahead of the hand who feeds him, for a good dog will always leave his food if he thinks there is sport in the offing!

The relationship between a man and his dog is closer than his relationship with any other animal. Few human relationships can match the love, trust, loyalty and unstinting performance which they share.

Alexander Mackay-Smith in
Foxhunting in North America

With three terriers in hot pursuit, this ground-hog climbed to what he thought was safety, 15 feet high in the tree. Soon the original three were joined by three more terriers who aggressively climbed up after him. Hard Sauce made it to the hog three times, with encouragement from a couple of the bitches. Fearing for their safety, HARD SAUCE having fallen out when bitten by the ground-hog, only to return to his tree climbing, the hunt was called off. This is not a Jack Russell's normal way of hunting—but it was quite a sight and quite a racket!

The author judging the final "cut" in a terrier class at the Canadian Fox Hound Show, London, Ontario, 1985.

Training and Showing Your Jack Russell Terrier

Wingate Mackay-Smith

In 1967 I got a call from a friend asking me to bring an entry to the terrier class at the Essex Hunt Puppy Show. It was the first time hunt terriers were to have their own class—great excitement! I agreed to go and then the fun started. First I had to find the two bitches. They eventually straggled in off the farm, hot, muddy and covered with ticks and burrs. After an hour or so of washing, plucking and de-ticking I had my two specimens ready. Little did I know how unready they were!

The older of the two, Buttercup, had never been in a car and neither of them had been on a lead. Buttercup responded to the lead like a clubbed seal, standing immobile with eyes raised in supplication to the Almighty. Arabella, on the other hand, gave a nifty rendition of a hooked marlin, which ended with a slipped collar and a dive under the porch. After a second trip to the wash-tub she and her mother were locked in a box-stall to await the dawn of SHOW DAY! So much for the training phase.

They both threw-up as we turned out of the driveway and we arrived in Far Hills thoroughly awash. It did give them the look of a genuine article, though, tucked up and hunting fit. In her class Buttercup crouched absolutely immobile and when asked to gait she permitted herself to be dragged, that was the sum total of her co-operation. In the next class, Arabella eventually stopped pitching about and, lured by an enormous sausage, managed to trot around the ring. Having parted with her breakfast on the ride over, she eventually decided she was very hungry, and stood gazing at the sausage in rapt concentration. She won the class and best bitch, but refused to chase the rat through the pipe and so surrendered her chance for Best in Show!

Well, I've learned a lot since then, although my showing experience has come with another breed of terriers rather than Jack Russells. The principles are the same though. The dog must be prepared for competition both physically and mentally, if it is going to do what is expected of it (which is win the class, of course!).

Puppies are most easily trained to lead between 10-16 weeks. It is usually easier if the leader has a long leash and some edible treat so the puppy thinks it is fun and rewarding to follow along (on the left side of the leader). If the puppy pulls back, give a tug, and as soon as it moves forward give it a snack. Soon it will be trotting along on a loose lead, head up and watching for its treat.

Next it should be trained to stand facing the handler and getting treats from time to time without jumping up. At first the handler must be quick to give a reward when the puppy is in the desired position, on all four legs on the ground and looking up. Since this is a fleeting moment at best with a puppy, you have to be quick. Later the puppy will stand for longer periods (several seconds) waiting for a bit of food. Extend the time with less frequent rewards until the dog will stand for 30 seconds or so. This can be done in the kitchen with odd scraps of food, or in the yard or tackroom with broken up dog biscuits.

Once the dog is trained to lead and bait it can be shown to advantage.

Handling the Jack Russell in the ring is not difficult, but it does require patience. Some dogs are natural showmen, others a bit uneasy in strange surroundings.

If your dog will gait and lead on a loose lead and stand and look at the bait when it is in the line up, you are well ahead of the game. You can show the dog on a loose slip-type lead with the lead loosely encircling the bottom of the neck, right at the shoulders. He should stand and stop squarely and require relatively little manipulation. He must be used to being touched by strangers as the judge will examine his teeth and probably will feel to see if he has "two of everything" behind. During this examination the lead should be held more tightly and the handler should maintain close control over the dog by bending down and holding the lead at the neck.

More nervous animals require a tighter lead and are less likely to want to take the bait. They sometimes settle down when they make friends with their next door neighbor in the ring and stand pretty well just watching another dog. The problem with this method ("baiting off other dogs") is that you have no control over the animal's attention. If the next-door dog is shy or unfriendly or its handler is either not interested in your problems or moves away, you are left with nothing to keep your dog alert and interested.

Gaiting the dog should be done at a medium trotting speed. This is the gait at which the dog looks his best. If the dog moves beside you on a loose lead without sniffing the ground or pulling to one side, it will give the best impression and allows the judge to assess his movement.

A few do's and don't's in the ring.

DO: Keep your eye on the judge and have your dog standing nicely and alertly when the judge is looking.

DO: Give your dog time to relax while the judge is examining other dogs.

DO: Watch the pattern of judging so when your turn comes you can show your dog with confidence and polish.

DON'T: Let your dog crowd and run up on other dogs in the ring. It not only messes up the other dog but distracts your own as well.

DON'T: Move your dog too fast. It's not a class for hovercraft.

DON'T: Expect to win with an untrained dog, no matter how good it is. You must have a good dog, in good condition and well presented, to be a consistent winner.

DON'T: feed good smelling morsels that might fall on the ground, causing the dogs coming behind to sniff the ground madly. And don't use squeaky or noisy toys to excite him which distracts the other dogs in the class.

The classes are much larger now than they were when Arabella followed the sausage around the ring. Competition is keen, and presentation is important if your dog is going to look his best.

Train him, condition him, present him. Your dog will enjoy the process, and you will enjoy the results!

"Even after three years, his intelligence continues to astound us."

A pleasant way for the terriers to wait their turn. It is more comfortable and relaxing than kennels. They can move about and talk to each other, have their beds to lie on, have fresh water and are staked out in the shade. The kennel at the back is made up of four sections hooked together so it can be carried in the trunk of a car and is fine for puppies up to 8-10 months (depending on the puppy!).

Another method of holding terriers at the show. I prefer the system in the above photo, providing the terriers accept it, and lie quietly, not charging at every dog or person that passes by! It is much cheaper (the stakes cost about $4.00!) and the dogs must be more comfortable. However, these kennels are next best, as they are open, getting any available breeze, and the terriers can see what's going on. These terriers belong to Terri Batzer.

General Health, Possible Problems and First Aid

The best health program for your dog is one where he is fed well and regularly, has a worming and immunization-shot schedule as set up by your veterinarian and, as much as possible, is never out of your (or someone's) sight when he is running free.

What he is fed is up to each owner. Dog people will argue all night about how much of this and that they should and shouldn't feed their dog. However, the simpler his rations, the better and healthier he'll be. Raw meat does not supply anywhere nearly all the "daily requirements." Tests conducted by leading dog food manufacturers have proved this beyond any doubt. On the other hand, many dry foods and a few canned foods do. If one brand of prepared food isn't agreeing with him (loose bowels, itching skin, loosing weight) don't be afraid to try another one. But don't resort to table scraps, unless they are mixed in with his regular feed, as they are not very nutritious and will take away his taste for his regular meals. Good hard bones are very important for clean teeth—knuckle bones (beef and ham), marrow bones and the usual hard man-made "dog bones" should be handed out regularly. It helps his breath, also!

One basic hazard for your terrier is his going-to-ground when you didn't see him, and getting stuck. If this might have happened, walk quietly around where he was last seen hunting, and LISTEN. Do NOT call his name. That will keep him from barking as he will stop to listen for you. No luck? Then the next thing is to start digging the holes where there has been some obvious activity around the opening (one that has a cobweb over it, would hardly be the place to look!). If you have a friend who has a go-to-ground terrier, get him to bring the terrier over and chances are he'll show you the hole where your terrier is stuck. We found Tamale that way, once. After sixteen hours, quite far from our house, Omelette (Tamale's great aunt!) kept going back to a small hole. We started digging (one has to dig very carefully because the ground might give away, filling up the hole and suffocating the terrier) and after an hour we found her stuck, head first in tree roots! Right ahead of her was a dead rabbit, who we guessed died of shock! She was released and she bounded away as if nothing had ever happened, and started hunting again! I don't think she lost a pound. The point is, don't give up looking; terriers have been known to live underground for two weeks. However, if Tamale hadn't been hunting, unsupervised, she wouldn't have been lost in the first place.

If you have to leave a collar on your terrier, cut the leather almost all the way through, or have an inch of elastic sewn into it, so if he becomes tangled or caught in something it will break or slip off.

Having your terrier tattooed is quite a deterrent to dog nappers. They find it hard to sell tattooed dogs to laboratories and pet dealers.

If you lose your terrier and suspect theft, call or write Action 81, Inc. at once. This non profit foundation operates as an International network to prevent and expose organized pet theft. Rt. 1, Box 151, Berryville, VA 22611, (703) 955-1278.

Keep his toenails cut! Letting them grow too long puts a terrible strain on his lower leg and makes him very flat footed. There is also the chance of one breaking off, causing great pain and excessive bleeding. Presumably, his dew claws were cut off when he was 3-5 days old.

Keep his ears clean and sweet smelling—any constant scratching and shaking of his head is likely to be caused from ear mites. Let your veterinarian have a look.

Puncture wounds can be washed out with hydrogen peroxide, using a small syringe and then some antibiotic squeezed into it. I keep a tube on hand, at all times. Open cuts can be cleaned with hydrogen peroxide and then sprayed with topazone. Penolog or Forte-Topical are excellent for cuts, puncture wounds, etc.

*WOODLUCK EGGBEATER at 15 years old before and after clipping. Clipping is good if your terrier has an extra heavy coat as it is easier to control fleas, ticks, skin irritation, etc. You clip in **the direction** of the hair growth, using large blades, so enough hair is left for protection against the sun and heat. A dog prespires through his mouth, his coat supplying insulation against the heat and the cold.*

Always good sports, these Jack Russell Terriers go along with the ride! From left to right, WOODLUCK EGGBEATER (out of sight behind horse's ears), WOODLUCK GRIDDLE, WOODLUCK SLURPY (lived to 18 years), WOODLUCK OMELETTE, WOODLUCK SAND-WICH, TEMPEST —with the author's three girls, Leslie, Denya and Caroline. (1976)

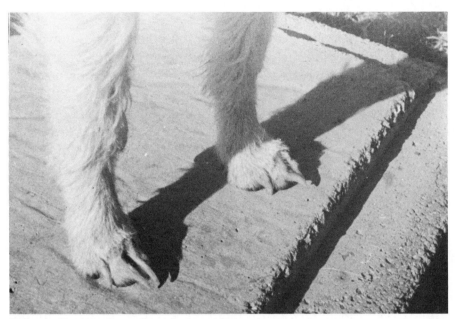

Toenails that have been allowed to grow far too long.

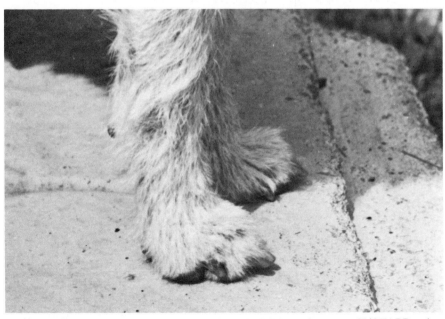

Same feet, after the toenails have been clipped. (With apologies to CUSTARD, who grew them as a demonstration for this book.)

When your dog develops itchy spots, or "hot spots," before spending many dollars on expensive remedies, baths, powders, pills, etc., try rubbing the spots with sulphur powder (available at your pharmacist) and lard (I use goose grease). Mix the powder with just enough lard to make a paste. Work it well into the afflicted areas—nine times out of ten it will do a great job. Repeat as needed. You can keep a jar of it in the refrigerator, with a tightly screwed on top, as it smells like rotten eggs! This is one of the "old time remedies" that is invaluable, which was shown to me by a gentle-man who has been breeding dogs (and horses) for over fifty years. (The same one who puts a large stone in the bottom of his puppies water bucket, so they can't knock it over!)

If your dog starts drooling and is not eating as he usually does—check inside his mouth. One thing that happens quite often, is that a stick becomes lodged between the upper teeth, across the roof of the mouth. From the outside, the mouth looks quite normal. Or he could have a loosened tooth, cut tongue, a bitten lip from a hunted varmint, and so on.

Terriers by nature, lock their jaws when they bite onto their quarry—this is their specialty. The lock is so strong, that human hands are unable to open the terrier's mouth. The same is true, if they get hold of a stick. So many times I have seen people showing off their dog, by swinging him, 2 or 3 feet off the ground, while he tenaciously holds on to a stick. It might be a marvelous show—but it is like spinning your wheels on dry pavement—it is wearing out the material. By doing this with a dog, you are causing his back teeth to loosen and they will eventually fall out. For the same reason, DON'T let them chase and/or pick up stones. Like the rubber on the tires, the front teeth are slowly being worn away—I have seen some that have been worn right down to the gums!

The normal temperature of a dog is 100.5° degrees to 102° degrees.

Poison is, unfortunately, often the cause of a dog's end. If your dog acts strangely or is having a seizure of any sort, RUSH him to the veterinarian, you might save his life. Don't wait to see if he is going to "come out of it." If you know he has eaten some poison (e.g., they love rat poison—don't ever put it where he can get to it) force him to swallow warm milk and plenty of salt, which will make him throw up. We saved four terriers this way—they had eaten over two pounds of mouse poison. The ten mile drive to the veterinarian would have taken too long, so we phoned him and he told us what to do. You should try forcing a Jack Russell Terrier to drink something he thinks is absolutely ghastly! It was a messy business—but it worked and they all survived!

Use a syringe to give medicine, an emetic (as above) etc.

In any case, any change of attitude or abnormal behavior on the part of your canine friend is to be observed very carefully and taken seriously. If it continues and you can't understand why, a visit to your veterinarian is imperative.

When traveling, fifteen minutes in a parking lot with a ball can get rid of lots of pent-up energy!

at least ninety-five percent of all Jack Russell terriers take to car riding.

Travel

One of the bonuses of owning a Jack Russell Terrier (there are so many!)—is his adaptability, which makes it fun to take him along, wherever you go. After his initial "car-ride" training, going with you in the car will be one of his most favorite pastimes. This "training" includes leaving him in the car while you shop, etc. without barking, jumping around, chewing or doing anything other than rest or look quietly out the window. The first step is to make a spot for him in the car, station wagon, truck, etc., where he can curl up and be comfortable. I use a piece of carpet that is cut the right size so it can be tucked under the back rest and cover the whole back seat. These can be obtained for little or nothing from your local carpet man who will have some odd pieces left over from a big job. When you need this area for passengers, take out the carpet and you have a clean seat! If I am going to be away from the car for a long period, I take the dog's bed along as well. This encourages him to settle and snooze while he is waiting for you.

First Car Rides

At least ninety-five percent of all Jack Russell Terriers take to car-riding, like ducks to water! There are a few, however, who for one reason or another, do get car sick. Possibly because when they were little fellows, their first couple of rides took them to the veterinarian—and their next one took them away from everything familiar, with no recognizable smells. (Remember the advice to give your puppy a sleeping pill or an anti-emetic when you brought him home from the breeder if he wasn't used to car travel.). It is advisable, therefore, to take the precaution of a very simple car riding training program.

For his first car rides, take his sleeping blanket, or doggie-bed, along, and some long lasting treats—such as boiled marrow bones, which are greaseless and last for hours. These first trips should be short—a mile or two, with a happy ending, such as a play in the park, a run on the beach, a picnic or just simply coming back home! If these are successful, make the rides longer. When your puppy is very young, I don't advise leaving him alone in the car, except for short periods (ten or fifteen minutes). If you have another dog with whom he's compatible, then he can be left for a little longer. As he gets older, you can lengthen the time accordingly—but be sure he has plenty of chew toys, for the sake of your car!

Your Jack Russell Terrier will not mind waiting 1-2 hours while you shop. He will feel the same about "his" car as he does about his den and probably will sleep all the time you are gone. Remember, if he is still a young puppy, to take him out for a short walk when you return to the car. If the day is going to be a long one, take along a bowl and some water in a jar, in order to be able to offer him small drinks. The collars (and leashes) of all the dogs in the car should be removed while they are alone, as they could become entangled by something, with serious results.

In the cold weather if you leave him in the car, be sure the windows are opened a crack and the car is parked in any available sun. In the warm weather, seek the shade (even if it means walking a little farther) and leave the windows open as far as possible without him being able to jump out. If the windows aren't partially opened, a dog can die very quickly from asphyxiation if the temperature is above 80°—many dog deaths are recorded each summer, due to the rapid rise in temperature in a closed up car.

Carsickness

If your Jack Russell Terrier, for whatever reason, does suffer from carsickness, it is worth the time and effort to try to find a cure—as he loves to be with you and go where you go. Also, there is no better lock for your car than a terrier who gives the appearance of wanting to shake up a possible thief as if he were a groundhog or stable rat!

Here is a programme that has worked for some dogs with this problem.

Step #1—Sit in the car with him for about ten minutes, with the windows open and offer him choice tidbits. The more relaxed *you* are the more likely your puppy will be relaxed. Take a book to read, or your needlepoint and act like nothing special was going on. Dogs take their cue from their handler. (If he is very nervous, consult your veterinarian about giving him a tranquilizer). Do this a few times, until he is relaxed and happy about being in the car.

Step #2—Put him in the car, by himself, with the radio on, the windows open a crack, and a few of his favorite treats. Leave him there for about 10 minutes. Praise him extravagantly when you take him out.

Step #3 & 4—Repeat steps one and two, only have the motor running.

Step #5—Take him for very short rides, praising and patting him all the time—100 yards is enough. Increase the distance each time until he becomes relaxed about it. Encourage him to lie down and be still, as charging around will only make him more excited. In these initial training stages don't worry about teaching him to stay in the back. That can be done when he can go for long rides without being sick.

These steps do not have to be done a day apart. You can do step one, for instance, two or three times in one day. As mentioned above, always have a joyous ending to the ride.

Some Guidelines to Happy Car Rides

Your terrier must have as good manners in the car as he does anywhere else. He must learn to be quiet—not to go leaping from the front to the back, and back to the front. He must learn NOT TO BARK with wild excitement, at any time. I had a letter not long ago from a lady who thought it was terribly funny because her dog loved to bark at every truck that went by! My guess is she didn't take the dog in the car very often—her head if not her nerves, wouldn't be able to stand it! My dogs are trained to stay in the back, when the car is moving. This is a safety precaution, e.g., they're not under your brake or sitting on the accelerator, or jumping in your lap unexpectedly, giving you a bad start—and so on. Your terrier must be taught to wait quietly in the car for your return and not bark non-stop. Continuous barking is very hard on him, as it keeps him in a state of nervous excitement. Also, it is most annoying for everyone else. If you are away from the car and hear him barking, get back to him as soon as you can, and give him a scolding. He will soon get the idea especially if he's learned the word "QUIET" at home. I have discussed how to teach him not to jump out of the car everytime you open the door, in the chapter "Basic Training."

If you stop at a motel or a friend's home you should be comfortable knowing that your terrier has been taught not to make a noise. I would like to point out that the time spent walking outside with your puppy and quietly waiting for him to "perform" during his house training days pays off when you're travelling. He will remember the lessons and will not take a long time to decide when and where to relieve himself! When he does, praise him and take him right inside, or back into the car. I train my dogs to the words "Good dog, good dog," saying them slowly and in a low voice (not the excited praise *"What* a good dog") when I am house breaking puppies—and they always remember what it means!

Long Trips

There is little to worry about if it is a Jack Russell Terrier you will be taking on a long trip—he is a marvelous, cheerful traveller and is especially good company when you are traveling alone.

We have discussed manners, barking and relieving himself—now all you have to do, is pack his "suitcase" and enjoy his company.

Here is a check list for "Static's" trip—
Collar and Leash
Water from his home in a jar—he is used to the taste, and will
    drink it more readily than strange water.
Canned food
Dry food
3 bowls—one each for water, for meals, and for free choice
Lots of Dog Biscuits
Chew toys
His own blanket or doggie-bed
Any medication he is taking

Flea powder—at this time of writing, the Zodiak line appears to be the most effective

Ear mite medication—Sometimes the terriers will pick up ear mites. A couple of treatments and all is well again.

Eye powder—You never know when he will get a scratch or a small infection in his eyes.

Some kind of wound powder

Penalog or Forte-Topical (marvelous for punctures, cuts, etc.)

Brush

And most important: A ball or whatever he will tear after and retrieve to you. This way, you can give him 15 minutes of hard exercise, whenever there isn't too much room to romp and play.

A metal spiral tether that can be screwed into the ground: If your puppy has been taught to lead, tie him to a tether, with a swivel attachment which keeps him from getting wound up around the post. This is a nice way to have him wait at a horse show, when everyone is trying to enjoy their picnic lunch, or at a terrier trials waiting for his classes and races. He can be in the shade and will be much cooler than waiting in a hot car. Remember to "stake him out" so he can't get caught or wound up in something, like another dog's line. Be sure he has access to plenty of fresh water.

Dogs, even Jack Russell Terriers differ in how much exercise they need when travelling. Mine show little interest in anything other than sleeping. They recognise the signs of a long trip—and settle down for a day of car riding. When we buy gas or stop for a meal I take them for walks and offer them water, and a few dog biscuits—naturally something is always saved from our meals as a treat for them! If your dog is restless, take him for a run with his ball or a stick and give him a good play, as well as a quiet time when he can relieve himself. Offer him water, but do not let him gulp down a whole bowl—you might get it back a little later. In the hot weather, if you don't have air conditioning make sure the temperature of your dog doesn't become so elevated that it turns into hyperthermia. If there are signs of this—excessive panting, glazed eyes, drooling (Jack Russell Terriers are not droolers) try to find a stream or lake and put him in it, getting him thoroughly wet. In any case, wrap him in a wet blanket or towel and rush him to a veterinarian.

Even plane travel from England to the U.S.A. can be fun for us little guys! Twelve week old "FAT CHANCE TRACTION" imported by Lynn Wade, Florida.

When driving with the windows open, do not let your dog put his head out, for many reasons; it is bad for his eyes and ears, a stone, a stick or some kind of debris could hit him, damaging his eyes or really hurting him; he could fall out if the car came to a sudden stop, he might jump out, etc.

Motels and Friends' Homes

The majority of motels today accept dogs, particularly if they are quiet. Some of them require a deposit, which they return to you after checking the room in the morning. However, once in a while you might check in at one that does not allow dogs. In this case, your dog will be perfectly satisfied to sleep in the car, especially if he has his own bed, some water and free choice food. Open one window a crack and lock the car. Most terriers would sound quite an alarm if anyone tried to break in! Be assured he is much more comfortable in the car, has a lot more room to move around, and is more familiar and relaxed with his surrounding than if he was in a cage at a boarding kennel with none of his loved ones nearby.

When you visit your friends on your trip, leave Static in the car until you have checked with them that it is all right to let him out. The reasons are too obvious to mention! If Static is as good and polite a guest as you are, you will both be welcomed back on your next trip and your host and hostess will remark on what mannerly dogs Jack Russell Terriers are!

Air Travel

Airplane travel is extraordinarily easy on dogs today. The rules and regulations have become so strict, that the airlines take great care of the traveler. There is no more leaving him in his kennel on a hot or cold windy airstrip. Federal regulations are exact on the temperature range they allow an airline to transport your dog (it has to be between 40° F and 85° F). They are loaded and unloaded by hand (no moving belts dump them into the baggage section— someone has to lift the kennel off and on the loader and in and out of the airplane) and they will agree to offer him water from time to time if he is on a long trip which requires a plane change. Shredded newspaper makes a great bed, and I always add a small piece of familiar blanket, for his reassurance! Stay at the airport until you are sure the plane is going to fly and then phone the recipient and tell him he's on his way. You will need a health certificate and, if he's over four months, a record of his rabies shot. A small amount of tranquillizer, as *recommended by your vet,* might make things easier for him. If he is a puppy going to a new home, he should have at least three days to acclimatize after arriving, before he goes anywhere—and then he should visit your veterinarian. Advise his new owners not to leave him at the vet's, unless it is an absolute emergency, because no matter how clean it is kept, there still will be lethal germs in the air to which the young puppy, no matter how well he is immunized, can be vulnerable.

Boating

Boating is a great joy for the Jack Russell Terrier. Before he has his first boat ride, make sure he knows how to swim. You have taught him to chase a ball and/or stick—so introduce him to water, when it is calm, by throwing a stick to the edge of it. As he gets his confidence (don't rush him, if he gets a scare he'll never get over it) throw the stick out a little further each time. Soon he'll be swimming like a retriever! Whatever you do, don't throw him in! When he is on the boat, he has to learn to be still—a boat, big or small, is no place for a dog to be running madly about, let alone barking wildly. Canoeing is one of our favorite things and both Tamale and Hard Sauce sit in the middle of the canoe, and fascinated, they watch the lake, lily pads, seagulls and fish slip by! If your terrier should fall overboard, get back to him immediately. Throw a life vest or preserver near him, he might grab hold of it, which could save his life. In cold salt water, you have NO time to loose. In fresh water, if he is a good swimmer, he can swim for quite awhile—so keep looking and encouraging!

"Hot C is doing wonderfully. We absolutely love him. He couldn't have two more devoted fans. My husband has always been a very narrow-minded fancier of the larger breeds, but he is as daffy about this pup as I am. He has been a perfect gentleman in the house."

Jack Russell Terriers are good swimmers. They have to be, as two of their favorite quarries are mink and otter. However, they must be properly introduced to water, as suggested in the chapter on travel.

Background
and History

Hunt Terrier Beginnings
A. Mackay-Smith

Dogs have been used to hunt game and vermin below ground since prehistoric times. In Oppian's "Cynegetica," written about 211 B.C., the author mentions "Agassoei, small and slender, used to follow beasts into their holes." An ordinance of Dagobert I, King of the Franks, dated 630 A.D., mentions "dogs which are called Bibarhunt, and which hunt underground." Edward, Second Duke of York (1373-1415), "Master of the Game and of the Hawks" to Henry IV in his translation from the French of Gaston Phoebus' Le Livre de la Chasse (1387) mentions "small curres that fallen to be terryers." Jacques du Fouilloux' "La Venerie et Fauconnerie" (1561), translated into English by George Turberville and published in 1575, in Chapter 65 speaks of two kinds of "terryers . . . to take the Foxe," the crooked legged, short haired breed of Flanders, and "another sorte there is which are shagged and streight legged (which) do serve for two purposes, for they wyll Hunte above the grounde as well as other houndes, and enter the earthe with more furie than the others."

We have to-day the same divisions among terriers, the rough and smooth coated, the short and long legged. In the first part of the 19th century, black and tan was the favorite color, but for the last hundred and fifty years or more, Masters have preferred white or nearly white dogs, such as Parson Jack Russell's famous bitch, Trump, with a bit of tan about the head and another tan spot just in front of the tail. During the 19th century terriers ran with the pack, so the long legged type was characteristic, but this practice was gradually discontinued because "they are apt to riot, and may go to ground in a big place and no one the wiser." Some of the larger English establishments still have a terrier man who rides at the rear of the hunt with the terrier in a leather bag, but the omnipresent Land Rovers and Jeeps are the most common means of transportation today.

Foxhunting in England serves the double purpose of providing sport and keeping the fox population within reasonable bounds. To accomplish the latter it is necessary to dig out foxes, so a terrier is required which will not fight the fox, but merely bark at it continuously so as to guide the diggers. In North America, on the other hand, where foxes are scarcer and do little damage, digging is almost unknown and terriers are maintained merely to bolt foxes in order to furnish additional sport.

What qualities should we require in a hunt terrier? It is a mistake to think that shortness of leg increases the terrier's ability to go to ground. It is the chest measurement that controls—no dog walks into an earth, he lies on his side and scratches his way in. Parson Russell liked his terriers about the size and shape of a vixen—14 inches high, 14 pounds in weight. Geoffrey Sparrow wrote: "I would have a dog weighing from twelve to sixteen pounds, with a strong jaw—not snipey like the show breeds—a good back, neck and shoulders, and fairly long legs. They can be folded up, while bad shoulders cannot. He must have plenty of heart room and throw his tongue well when up to his game."

Colonel Sparrow, author of The Terrier's Vocation (1940), hunted with The Crawley and Horsham for many years. He was particularly keen not only about painting and drawing, but also about working terriers.

John Emms—1899

The Earth Stopper and his Terriers. *Earths (fox holes) are located by a man (earth stopper) with the help of his terriers the night before the next day's fox hunt, with hounds. If the terriers bark, the earth stopper leaves that hole open, because there is a fox in it. If they don't bark, it is filled loosely with 2 or 3 shovels of dirt so that the hunted fox cannot go to ground. After the hunt, the fox easily unstops the earth. Notice the resemblance of these terriers to many bred in England and North America to-day.*

John Emms (1843-1912) loved to paint fox hounds. In his paintings of hounds in kennels or around the stable yard he nearly always included a terrier or terriers. They would be white with a small amount of black or brown and have a rough coat. Needless to say, it is this type of hunt terrier which to-day carries the name of Jack Russell Terrier.

HARD SAUCE, BOING and TAMALE at Windmill Point, Virginia.

Chipmunk? Squirrel? Rattlesnake? "Gone to Ground" on an island in Georgian Bay, Ontario, Canada.

Dozer & Friends. *This painting, by Jamie Wyeth is not only of his terrier, but also includes his wife driving her Welsh pony.* (Copyright Jamie Wyeth)

By William Barraud 1810-1850. A couple of Lord Henry Bentinck's Fox Hounds with a Terrier.
(Oil on canvas 44 × 56 c. 1845 Courtesy of Paul Mellon, Upperville, Virginia)

What Makes a Hunt Terrier?
A View From England

Mary Roslin-Williams

I have written articles on Foxhounds and hunting in England, giving the difference between the south country orthodox method and type of hounds, and the mountain and moorland hunting, with their completely different type of hound. Each is suitable for its own terrain, the southerners being mounted and the others hunting on foot.

There is a complete dividing line between them, depending on whether you roused your fox from his day-bed in covert (south country) or whether you dragged the overnight line until you found his day-bed in a clump of rushes or a bracken-bed up on the Fells (north county).

Exactly the same clear-cut division stands between the south country hunt terrier and the north country one, only in this case there is not only north and south, but the north is again divided, making a large section down south and two smaller but equally important ones up north, i.e. the north-west and the north-east, the Pennines separating them.

The reason for these differences is that just as the hound-work is different, so also is the terrier work.

Main Difference

First I will explain the main difference in the work. The big foxhunting establishments, down south, will have an official terrier man. Unfortunately he often is hindered by well-meaning spectators and car-followers who own a terrier of some sort and wish to have a try. These are often hated by the professional huntsman, who has his job to do and who wants to get on with it, and not waste time with what he considers half-baked terriers and clueless handlers.

Then, there is the quiet, tweedy man, standing in the right place, with two or three narrow-shouldered, varminty, white terriers of the right shape and size for the country hunted. Both man and dogs are thoroughly experienced and totally trusted by the hunt staff. These are worth their weight in gold to a hardpressed huntsman.

The official terrier man has a batch of similar terriers, also thoroughly experienced, and these do the bulk of the terrier work all day and indeed every hunting day. His terriers are those small, white, often smooth but usually broken-coated dogs we call south country hunt terriers. Then the general public got hold of them, thickened their shoulders and called them erroneously "Jack Russells." Poor Jack Russell, his grave must by now be like a mole hill from him turning over in it!

Then and Now

In the old days the terrier man often rode with his terriers slung in a bag from his saddle. Now, more often, he travels by car, nicking in when wanted and then walking to the earth where the fox has gone to ground. Here the first and biggest difference between the northern and southern divisions occurs.

Down south the subscribers to a hunt want a good gallop across a lovely rolling riding country, with attractive fences and rails to jump and a point of about four miles at least, if not a lot more. The idea is to find the fox lying above ground in a warm covert, rouse him and let him get a very good start (giving him law is the technical term) and then, having gathered all the pack, to hunt his line perhaps a quarter of a mile behind him while he makes for one of his safety-holes, perhaps four or five miles away.

When he gets there, all the nearer holes having been stopped (filled in) the night before, he dives to earth and the Master of Hounds then decides whether he must be dug out and killed because he is a known hen or turkey killer, or whether he is left to live, being a good, straight necked fox.

Never Kills

If he has to be killed because he is a chicken killer, or some such nuisance, the terriers are called in. They go down to him, very often in a small rabbit hole, hence the necessity of narrow clean shoulders, and mark the fox, which does not include biting him; but merely means barking at him constantly, so that the terrier man can dig down and get the fox out. *The south country terrier never kills.* If the fox finds a small rabbit hole, immediately after being found in his original bed, he is bolted by these yapping terriers, whereby he gives a hunt.

The south country terrier is small so that he can be carried if necessary. He must be narrow-shouldered so that he can get in where a very narrow-shouldered fox can enter, but need not have long legs to hamper him when put into an earth starfish fashion. This makes it difficult to put him in the hole, because his long legs stick out and push against the sides, so that he hurts himself. *(Ed. note—an enthusiastic, well trained terrier, would not do this, in any case. Today, long legs are not considered to present any problems when putting a terrier to ground.)*

Last but certainly not least, he is white because he very often has to bolt his fox, and if in south country sandy soil he comes out behind his fox, sandy-coloured and SMELLING OF FOX, he may easily be chopped (killed with no preceeding run) by hounds, in error.

North Country Terrier—A Different Job

Now we come to the north country terrier which has a different job with foxhounds. He is not called a north country hunt terrier to match his south country confrere, because he is either a Border or a Lakeland type. This is because, although the type of hunting is the same, there is a different purpose in the west (Lakeland) and the east (Northumberland).

In Lakeland and Northumberland the foxes are rogues. They do terrible damage to lambs, being a larger type than the little red south country fox. They are called a greyhound fox, being bigger, leggier, with a longer, more loping stride, than his south country brother. He lies out on the mountainsides, usually above ground.

The night-before's drag (the line the fox made while moving around for food, etc.) is hunted, until the fox jumps up from his bed, in front of hounds, and sets off for his long run. Very seldom does he have to be bolted first. Then the terriers come more into their own, when he eventually goes to ground.

WOODLUCK OMELETTE and WOODLUCK TAMALE take to jumping into water, after sticks, like any seasoned labrador retriever!

Although not bred to mark quarry in trees, a Jack Russell Terrier is so enthusiastic and intent on his hunt, that he doesn't stop even when the going gets tough!

A Working Terrier

"Jack Russell" Is Type of Working Terrier
Bred and Used by The Reverend John Russell

by Ralph Greaves

The term "Jack Russell," if it means anything, can only mean the type of working terrier that was bred and used by the Reverend John Russell of Iddesleigh, Devonshire, who kept his own pack of hounds and hunted the North Devon country from about 1820 to 1883—and that is a very long time ago.

Parson Russell's name is still a legend, for a better and more honoured sportsman never lived, nor a more successful Master of Foxhounds in a wild and difficult country. He was famous for his dwarf foxhounds, but he was even more famous for his hunt terriers, which he bred himself.

The question then arises as to how they were bred, and what they were like. There is no doubt at all they were bred primarily for work; and it follows that a terrier, to be good in his work, must, like the foxhound, have certain physical, besides temperamental, qualifications. In the course of some fifty years therefore, Parson Russell's terrier kennel, probably after a lot of very close breeding, had a definite family stamp or resemblance, which produced and established a pronounced strain of working terrier.

A "strain," however, is by no means the same thing as a "breed." The latter, to gain recognition, must be firmly stabilised by means of a Stud Book; while a strain, however carefully guarded by its originator during his lifetime, will eventually work itself out. Can anyone claim that Parson Russell's strain has been preserved through all the ensuing generations, and if so, what evidence can they produce? It is conceivably possible that someone in the West Country might be able to prove a line back to the Iddesleigh terriers of the sixties or seventies of last century; but it would be exceedingly difficult in the absence of a Stud Book. One line by this time would have worn exceedingly thin.

The Original Article

And what were Parson Russell's terriers really like? In Fores' Guide to the Hounds of England published in 1850, there is an account written by one who actually visited the kennels and saw the terriers, when the strain had been established for a number of years. The writer dwells chiefly on their working qualities, of which he gives an interesting account, but from his general description one also gets a clue to their appearance.

"They are invariably white," he remarks, "half-faced with black, or having just a black ear, a little wiry about the muzzle, with a remarkably clean head; pricky in the ears *(author's note: in the 1850s this would describe ears that are erect and folded over, not standing straight-up like a German Shepherd's ears)* and straight in the limbs." I have found, too, another description, this time of Parson Russell's first bitch, which be bought from a milkman when an undergraduate at Exeter College, Oxford. Her name was Trump, and she was white, with dark patches on head and ears, and one at the root of her tail. Her coat is described as thick, close, and a little wiry; she was on straight legs, was narrow in the chest, and her weight was about fourteen pounds.

There are two points to notice in the above descriptions. Firstly that both writers describe the coat as a little wiry, one applying this description to the muzzle only. The inference is that the coat was of the short variety, harsh and probably broken, but neither silky nor wooly. The sort of coat, in fact, that a working terrier requires, is one that sheds water. The heavy, soft coat, so often exhibited by the distant Jack Russell of today, is the most unsuitable, getting caked with mud, which the dog is unable to shake off, and adding unnecessarily to the weight which he has to carry around. The second point is the narrow chest—absolutely essential in a working terrier that has to go underground, where a broad-chested dog will indubitably get stuck. A terrier should be able to pass through a nine-inch drain pipe, and it is the width of the chest rather than the length of the leg that is the deciding factor.

Known By Their Work

We have then, a fairly authentic picture of the Jack Russell as he really was. The impression one gains is rather of the old English terrier which one sees in sporting prints.

As regards the working qualities of Parson Russell's terriers, one cannot do better than quote from the writer who actually saw them; "They run with the hounds" he tells us, "and while the latter are drawing the deep coverts, they draw the deep earths, with which that country abounds; thus the labour and expense of stopping is at once rendered unnecessary. In chase they are always on the line, and when a check occurs, if a fox is suspected of having gone to ground, they are sure to be there to settle the question, ere the first cast has been accomplished."

Parson Russell is quoted as giving a remarkable description of the sagacity of one of his old favourites, Tip by name, who seems to have had all the instincts of a good whipper-in when hounds were running. "Old Tip was far more useful in my wild country," Mr. Russell says, "than the best earth-stopper. If he found a fox was pointing for any of the strong earths (for he knew them all), he used to 'get on' with all speed and endeavour to 'shut him out.' Standing like a champion on top of the earths, he would prick his ears in the direction of the coming pack, throw his tongue with all energy and defy, as loudly as he could, the enemy to approach his strong, and perhaps inaccessible holt. Many a run has been gained, and many a fox killed by his timely intervention." Tip, we are told, through many seasons, never missed a day. He never seemed to tire, though he frequently went fifteen or twenty miles to covert with hounds before the day's hunting had even begun.

Parson Russell's terriers apparently had the run of the house, and were his "fireside friends," receiving as much consideration as the most favoured of his guests. He primarily bred them for their work, which they did superbly, and were, in fact, just a family of first-class working terriers.

The Chronicle, October 31st, 1952

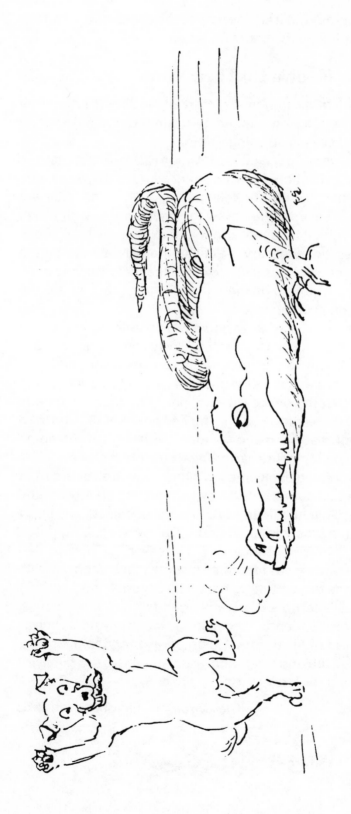

"He's afraid of nothing, or no-one or no beast."

Two styles of race course. The closed-in track is the one that fulfills the racing rules of the J.R.T.C.A.

FOXWARREN NETTLE—owned by Paul Ross. A lovely, balanced bitch. At the time of writing this book, there are only a few Jack Russell Terriers under twelve and a half inches who are well balanced (length of back, from base of withers to base of tail, is the same as from the top of the withers to the ground). Note the good size bone and the power in the forelegs and hindquarters, and how close to the ground her knees and hocks are. She has a grand head, with a nice arch to her neck. Her chest span is 15".

MEYNELL REMUS. Imported from England by Mary Johnson, Vermont, where he took fourth in the 1984 British Nationals. He stands 14½ inches, but his get have not been that tall. A good example of a broken coat.

The Fox Terrier Connection

Paul F. Ross

Most people seem to have heard that the Jack Russell Terrier was bred by the English Parson, the Reverend John Russell. What most people do not know, is why he was bred as he was, or what he should really look like in order to be called a Jack Russell Terrier. The facts gathered here come, not only from modern but also more importantly, from older books, written in the period when the terrier was at its height, the years from 1830 to 1900. Some information is also taken from a book on Hunt Terriers by Jocelyn Lucas, published in 1931, a sort of mid-period in the Jack Russell Terrier's history.

Many different types of terriers were, and still are, used to go to ground on fox in England. After 1805, avid fox hunters decided they could improve upon the then, mostly used, black and tan colored Fox Terrier. One of the major problems they thought was its color, so easily mistaken for a fox and not easily seen in a dig. At that time the black and tan terrier, rather like a Manchester type terrier, or a rougher version like the Fell or Welsh Terrier, was probably the most commonly used for fox. The English White Terrier (now extinct) was also a terrier that had gained some popularity, some say due to his very friendly nature. It is almost certain that a combination of these two terriers developed into the

Jack Russell, or more correctly, the working Fox Terrier of pre-1900. There is no doubt John Russell at first only bred what was known then as the Fox Terrier, and later it was developed into what we now call the modern Fox Terrier. This fact is documented in old and modern books on the Fox Terrier. (*reference—see end of chapter*). John Russell himself was a founder member of the English Kennel Club, and at times judged the Fox Terrier classes for this organization. Quite a few offspring of John Russell's own terriers became famous Fox Terrier bench champions of the English Kennel Club. As observed by some authorities, terriers of the Jack Russell type had already been accepted and recognized by the Kennel Club, as far back as about the early 1870's! Of course John Russell was but one of many who were breeding the Working Fox Terrier of the pre-1880 period. His terriers became famous; not only did they have great intelligence and working ability, but they were also extremely good looking dogs.

Conformation and purity of blood were very important to John Russell. Some writers credit mixes of Beagle, Greyhound, Dachshund, and Bull Terrier in the make-up of the Jack Russell Terrier. This is almost certainly true of some of the modern Hunt Terriers and many of the terriers that in modern times have been given the name of Jack Russells just because they were mainly white in color! But this was not the way of John Russell's breeding. It is documented that John Russell hated the Bull Terrier cross in his or any fox terriers. It made them too hard for their work, and often mute when they went to ground. Well before 1880, brindle coloring, indicating the Bull Terrier cross, was mentioned in the Kennel Club standard of the Fox Terrier as undesireable. John Russell is credited as keeping his breeding quite pure, with the admitted exception of two stud dogs, namely Old Jock and Tartar. A letter written by Russell to a Mr. Wooten on March 13, 1867 shows what he thought of Jock:

> *"I never saw a sweeter animal than Jock, so perfect in shape, with so much quality. He is as near perfection as we poor mortals are ever allowed to feast our eyes upon. His temper is so beautiful and his pluck undeniable, for I choked him off a dog fox."*

The dogs in the illustration of Jock, Grove Nettle and Tartar (Illus. 1), are considered by most authorities to be the foundation stock of the modern Fox Terrier.

The Lucas book, however, states rumors had it that Parson Russell would take in any terrier coming up to his demandingly high standards. This also could be true, for he could have used

JOCK. GROVE NETTLE. TARTAR.
Illustration 1

Illustration 2

photo by Gary Scott Breithaupt
The photographer's Jack Russell Terrier PATCH still full of plan at seventeen years old.   She lived to be eighteen, just as her father did!

these dogs to help his work in the field, and not necessarily for breeding with his own strains.

In any case, Russell's terriers were in great demand. Even later, when the modern Fox Terrier became more prominent, his blood lines were highly respected and bragged about, if present in one's pedigree. Modern books on the Fox Terrier, give John Russell most of the credit for the breeding of the rough coated Fox Terrier, stating that his conscientious and pure breeding were responsible for this fine animal. So much for the few who credit Russell's terriers as being wonderful mongrels!

What did John Russell's terriers look like?

In spite of the variations of sizes and shapes seen today in dogs that take the name of Jack Russells, there is no doubt, by looking at the various old prints (not just Trump!) and descriptions of the parson's terriers, what they looked like, and still do. (See the chapter A Working Terrier, by Ralph Greaves, page 141). He preferred his terriers about the size of an adult fox: fourteen inches at the shoulder, around fourteen pounds in weight, and quite high on the leg. These terriers had to follow the hunt on foot, they were rarely carried around on horseback. That practice seemed to become popular at a later date. Fourteen inches at the shoulder does not mean a large dog, and fourteen pounds is not heavy at that height. In fact, like a fox, these terriers were, if anything, quite slim. To give some idea as to this ideal size of terrier, a fourteen to sixteen inch chest was probably a preferred requirement.

To sum up, the true Jack Russell Terrier of yesteryear and today is without doubt the Fox Terrier as he was pre-1880 or thereabouts.

The modern Fox Terrier (as recognised by the English and American kennel clubs) (See Illus. 2) has changed from this working dog into a show dog. The major changes are first of all, his size, making him too big to go to ground. Another change, easily noticed, is his head, which is very different to that of his working ancestor. The head of the modern Fox Terrier is extremely long and narrow, unlike the working Fox Terrier of old, whose head was shorter and broad to accommodate his brain and jaw power, which is now legendary. The coat of the rough type Fox Terrier has also changed, from a broken type coat to one that can look like a sheep's when unclipped. The modern Fox Terrier now appears as a Picassoism of the true Working Fox Terrier—now known as the Jack Russell Terrier.

Other terriers that have also stood the test of time and are the most commonly used in the hunting of foxes today, are the Lake-land Terrier, the Border Terrier, the Fell and Patterdale Terriers. All these terriers have good legs and balanced bodies. The reason for fairly short backs, and a flat chest and rib cage, is that it gives the terrier an untiring maximum stride, so he can travel long distances and keep up with hounds. Flexibility and small chests allow terriers to follow the fox in tight places underground.

North America and the Jack Russell Terrier

It is certain that the Jack Russell Terrier was in the United States well before the 1920's. Today in North America, the terrier is rarely used with fox hounds, as organised hunts that chase live fox, (rather than drag line), often end the hunt when the fox goes to ground, as they do not wish to kill a good running fox, but want to save him for another day. Captain Jocelyn Lucas, who wrote *Hunt and Working Terriers,* pub. 1931, writes that when he visited the States in this period, the trend of not killing the fox had already started. Grey foxes are native to Canada and the United States, but red foxes are native only to Canada and the northern tier of the United States. There is no early evidence of red foxes from New Jersey south. English red foxes were imported during the 18th century to the Eastern Shore of Maryland, a frequently mentioned date is 1730. When the Chesapeake Bay froze over during the hard winter of 1779-1780, descendants of the imported foxes crossed on the ice and spread gradually south and west, reaching Georgia in the 1840's and Kentucky about 1850. Unlike hounds in English fox hunts, hounds in American packs are rarely blooded.

Lucas tells of the various types of terriers used by the American hunts in the 1920s. Here are two examples. The Myopia Hunt of Essex County, Massachusetts, used a Sealyham-Fox Terrier cross, with a dash of White Bull Terrier. The terriers were used for flushing and killing fox, from drains and woodchuck holes. This hunt usually kept two terriers which ran with hounds. The Star Ridge Hunt, which was in New York State (established 1928) used Jack Russell Terriers that had pedigrees going back to John Russell's own strain. They liked a very slim type, as most foxes took refuge in woodchuck holes. This hunt carried their terriers on horseback.

Surprisingly enough, terrier trials were also fairly common in the United States in the 1920's. Photographs in Lucas' book show Jack Russell type terriers, with good legs and balanced frames, worrying a woodchuck at one of these trials. Here is how the book describes these trials and the terriers, obviously true type foxhunting terriers of the traditional size.

"In America, terrier trials are sometimes held on woodchuck. The terrier has to show itself keen to get to ground, and must kill the woodchuck when he is dug out. The hole is too small for a dog to go down, so that the trials are of necessity a little artificial. Woodchucks are, however, game fighters with good teeth."

It is sure, as long as foxhunting remains legal in the British Isles, the Jack Russell type of terrier will always keep the beauty, balance and perfection that John Russell had in his terriers. Our modern, professional terrier men will see to that. Of course, there are many terriers who are called Jack Russells, whose only resemblance, to the parson's true type of working Fox Terrier is the head and coloration.

John Russell's type terrier has been used all over the world, to hunt all manner of game; such as rats, woodchuck, badgers, jackals, antelopes, warthogs, leopards, wild boar, coyote, etc. Parson John Russell and his contemporaries, not only produced a perfect animal for the hunting of fox, but one that has shown itself adaptable to all types of game. We have available the best all round working terrier in the world, and we must continue the effort to preserve the traditional type of Jack Russell Terrier strain.

Suggested reading for further history:

Pub. 1975 All About the Jack Russell. Mona Huxham
   (Reprinted and still available)
Pub. 1931 Hunting and Working Terriers. Capt. J. Lucas
   (Reprinted and still available)
Pub. 1900 The Fox Terrier. Hugh Dalgeil
Pub. 1902 The Fox Terirer. Rawdon B. Lee
Pub. 1924 Working Terrier. J. C. Briston-Noble
Pub. 1904 With Hound and Terrier in the Field. Alys F. Serrell
Pub. 1879 The Classic Encyclopedia of the Dog. Vero Shaw
   (Reprinted and still available)

"I have given many gifts over the years, but none will ever top the one I gave my husband last Christmas. Tiger is the smartest, happiest, bounciest creature we have ever known; with a personality that totally captures everyone who meets him."

Any swimming pool is better than none in Thomasville, Georgia in the summer! Owned by the famous horse show rider and judge, Jane Womble. The ears are just barely acceptable—they should be lying down, close to the head.

I've got it!

Terriers in the USA and Canada After World War II

Terriers have been used by sportsmen in the South Eastern U.S.A. and the Mid-Eastern section of Canada to mark and bolt foxes and various species of varmint since the 1940s.

Ben Hardaway, well known Master of Foxhounds (Midland Hunt, Georgia) and past president of the Masters of Foxhounds Association has owned and bred terriers since 1957 for the express purpose of marking or bolting foxes. Nearly all terrier breeders, in the south, have Hardaway breeding in their lines. Being a good judge of animals (dogs, hounds, horses, etc.) he has bred good looking terriers, both rough and smooth coated, and kept detailed accurate breeding records.

Another important post World War II breeder is Dr. Molly Donahue (a veterinarian) now of Charlottesville, VA. who, like Hardaway, has kept precise stud books. She imported her first terrier from the Fitzwilliam Hunt, England, in 1961 (Jack Russell in type—there were no clubs or associations in those days) and these dogs, plus others of hers are found in many extended pedigrees. For two decades her breeding has been sought after, as it has a great reputation for terriers who are excellent working underground. Dr. Donahue was a close friend of Sir Jocelyn Lucas (quoted earlier in this book) and bought several dogs from him.

In Canada the Eglinton Hunt (Toronto), the Toronto North York Hunt, (Aurora, Ont.) and the Montreal Hunt (Quebec) all have kept hunt terriers with hounds, as far back as 1939, up until the present day. The Hamilton Hunt also boasts terriers which they have had since 1955. Phylis Rawlinson a member of the Toronto North York Hunt and enthusiastic foxhunter for over 60 years, imported a white terrier from England, in 1939. A friend of her father's, who at that time was well advanced in years, urged her to buy one of his terriers. Miss Rawlinson declined because the bitch had some brown on her back, and she wanted an almost white one. More's the pity—as they were direct decendants of the Parson Jack Russell's dogs, the man's father having been a close friend of the Parsons! Indeed, she remembers many pictures of them both, with their terriers. What a gold mine was missed in this case! At that time, the white terriers with some brown or black, were not called Jack Russell Terriers, but Hunt Terriers or White South Country Terriers.

Nancy Gerry Bedford then living in Toronto, Ont. imported terriers from the famous Firhill Kennels in England as early as 1958 (a bitch and a dog) and continued adding English lines to her breeding, up until 1970.

For many years after World War II (well into the 60's, the Hunters' Horn, a monthly magazine for field trial foxhounds, advertised "DEN dogs" for sale, which could well have been loosely called Jack Russell Terriers, and who were sold all over the Eastern States.

While Mrs. Philip Fanning was Master of the Essex Foxhounds she imported white terriers from England and Ireland. Like your author, she got her first bitch from Bert Pateman, kennel huntsman to the Duke of Beaufort (Gloucestershire, England). This was a tri-colored terrier which she bred to a Norwich Terrier. As long as she was Master she continued breeding these terriers, which were predominately white. She is historically important as she sold Mrs. Ailsa Crawford, President and Founder of the J.R.C.T.A., her first white terrier! She also held one of the first terrier classes at hound shows in 1967. That same year your author persuaded Mr. William Brainard, ex M.F.H., President of the Virginia Foxhound Club, and organizer of its show held at Glenara, Marshall, Virginia to hold terrier classes. As far as I can ascertain these two shows were the first such classes ever held at hound shows in the U.S.A. since the 1920s. They were an overnight success!

mentioned here. Primarily they keep terriers for their own purposes and do not need to show or breed on a formal basis, but have
marvelous sporty dogs. These are the backbone of the terrier, as
they are bred strictly for their courage, personality and working
qualities. As long as there are sportsmen such as these, the Jack
Russell Terrier will never become a useless show dog—with perfect conformation and not much else. Fortunately, each dog is
registered with the J.R.T.C.A. ON HIS OWN MERIT, which allows a
dog with one registered parent to be registered, provided the other
parent is a good working terrier and he himself conforms to the
breed standard.

The Jack Russell Terrier Association of Great Britain was
founded in 1975 and the Jack Russell Terrier Club of America 1976.
Since then, a dog, providing he meets certain criteria, can be
registered with a Jack Russell Association and called a Jack Russell Terrier. Before this time, no one can claim breeding or owning
"A Jack Russell Terrier." They could claim breeding or owning a
type or strain—that's all. What was bred in England, Ireland and Scot-
land and/or imported to the U.S.A. and Canada, previously, was
properly referred to as a White Hunt Terrier. It will take a few more
years before Jack Russell Terriers will, again, resemble the type of
dog the Parson bred and hunted. One sees more and more of them
to-day; but there are still hundreds of white terrier type dogs, with
some brown splashed on them, that are incorrectly called Jack
Russell Terriers. They are super little dogs, full of personality,
gameness and courage and only are separated from the Jack
Russell Terrier, because their conformation does not conform to
the breed standard as laid down by the respective associations in
the U.S.A. and England. Nor do these bear much resemblance to
the working, white terrier of the nineteenth century.

*"I can't begin to tell you what a treasure Merlin is. I've had several
dogs and many other pets over the years but Merlin is by far the most
delightful animal I have ever known . . . He is very intelligent, was
easily house broken and responded almost immediately to the simple
commands of NO, SIT and STAY."*

MARKING ─────────────────────

ABOVE GROUND

A beautiful pair of under 12" terriers. NETTLE and NIPPER, owned by Mr. and Mrs. Christopher Howells (He is huntsman for the Blue Ridge Hunt, Millwood, Va.). These terriers were shown extensively at terrier trials in Maryland, Virginia, Pennsylvania and North Carolina. If one was champion, the other would be reserve. They were an unbeatable combination as long as they were shown!

The Jack Russell
Terrier in America

A Message From the President of the Jack Russell Terrier Club of America

As Founder and President of the Jack Russell Terrier Club of America, I am most fortunate in knowing and having as friends many owners of this exceptional breed. This first American book about the Jack Russell Terrier, written by Marilyn Massey (better known as Marilyn Mackay-Smith), a staunch supporter, Judge, member of our club and breeder of twenty years, will give to the reader an insight into this wonderful dog. By the time you have finished reading it, you will, I am sure, have experienced all the emotion I and many others have experienced over the years of knowing and owning Jack Russell Terriers.

The J.R.T.C.A. was formed in 1976 for the major purpose of preserving the quality of the breed, and to provide a central registery for the benefit of serious Jack Russell Terrier owners and breeders. It is completely dedicated to that purpose. Club membership is rapidly increasing along with the growing interest in Jack Russell Terriers in the U.S.A. and Canada. The club now has many dedicated people throughout the country working to achieve club goals. There is a growing list of A & B conformation and working judges, and representatives are being added from all states, as well as committees. As of 1985, the Club has a Board of Directors, whose main goal is to work together with judges, representatives and committees to preserve the conformation, working qualities and character of this wonderful terrier, and maintain close liaison with owners, breeders and interested people from their respective areas.

The Jack Russell Terrier Registry is closely controlled and requires many things to protect the breed that other Registeries do not. Up to date records are kept on each terrier registered. Show and working records are recorded, and terriers are not accepted for registration with any inherited abnormalities that could be passed on to future generations. Inbred terriers (as opposed to line bred) are turned down for registration.

I have always believed that to have a strong breed organization, there must be one central club in which everybody works together with understanding, devotion, intelligence and strong commitment to its goals. They must have the breed qualities and standards at heart; and a completely unbiased, unselfish commitment to it and above all else, strive to preserve its unique properties. After nine years in business, I feel we have just such an organization in the Jack Russell Terrier Club of America, thanks to our very supportive Board of Directors, Committees, Representatives, Judges, club members, owners and breeders.

Ailsa M. Crawford 1985
Founder and President
the Jack Russell Terrier
Club of America, Inc.

"She is one of the nicest dogs anyone could ever own . . . she is very obedient. I will guarantee a more intelligent one has never been bred."

This nine month old puppy is not balanced, as his back measured from the base of the withers is noticeably longer than the length from his withers to the ground (e.g. shoulder and leg). It is possible that he will outgrow this, and become a well balanced mature dog.

MEGAN, bred by Marsha Corum and owned by Judy Breuer, Pennsylvania, has been successful in her 1985 puppy showing.

Photo courtesy of National Sporting Library

Ray Pearson, who for many years was huntsman for the Old Domin-ion Hunt, Virginia. He is holding his famous terrier MINOR, who was literally unbeaten in conformation hunt terrier classes at the Fox Hound Shows. He is an excellent type and is found in many Jack Russell Terrier pedigrees, especially in the South. Here MINOR is receiving his championship trophy at the Virginia Fox Hound Show.

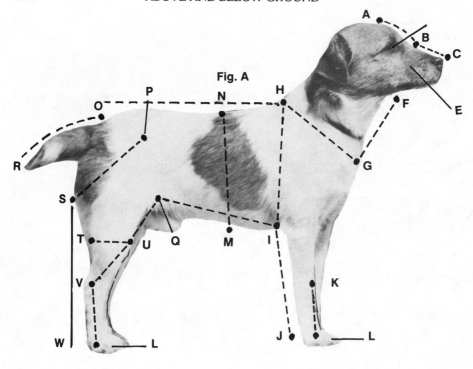

Fig. A

A skull flat, not pointed.

B defined stop, but not too much.

B to C is slightly shorter than **B to A.**

D eye is almond shape and dark.

E good depth through jaw.

F to G good length of neck.

G to H good slope of shoulder.

H to I and **I to J** are equal length, but some terrier men like the leg, **I to J,** a little longer than **H to I,** but it *never* should be shorter.

H to I good depth through the girth allowing for lung room.

K to L should be short.

L feet round and up on toes.

H to O same length as **H to J.**

I to Q good bottom line, with slight arch to loin **(Q).**

N to M Fairly flat ribs, slightly narrower than depth through girth.

P to S good length from point of hips to point of buttocks.

O to R should be 4 inches long, set fairly high and carried away from body.

S to W *when standing square,* the point of the buttocks, hocks and leg from hocks to the back of the feet should touch an imaginary perpendicular line.

V to U the line from **V to U** is at a good angle to the line from **V to W.**

V to W should be short. e.g. **V to W** should be half of **V to Q.**

T to U should be wide (from the side) powerful, but not bulging.

The lower leg from the knee to the ground, **K to L;** and from the hock to the ground, **V to W** should be straight and should be perpendicular to the ground—as viewed from any angle.

A to B slightly shorter than **B to C**.

D almond shaped, dark, bright eye.

E good depth through jaw, which is powerful.

F to G and **H to I**, not too wide.

J flat shoulders.

K to L same length as **L to M. L to M** can be slightly longer than **L to K,** but must never be shorter.

N to O short. Desirable is that **N to O** is ½ of the length from **N to P.** (e.g. knees to top of foot, versus knees to elbows.)

P, N, O elbows, knees and feet in a straight line, which is perpendicular to the ground.

R good round feet with toes reasonably tight to-gether.

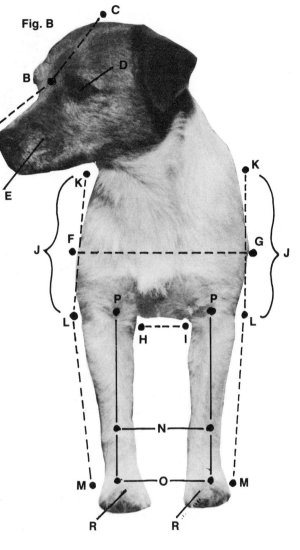

Fig. B

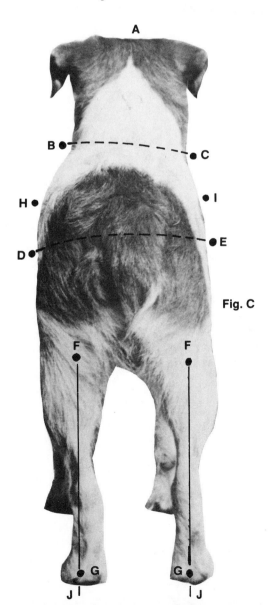

Fig. C

A flat, not domed head.

B to C not wide or heavily muscled neck and shoulders. Shoulders are flat, not bulging out.

D to E plenty of width between hips, allowing for freedom and strength in the hindquarters.

H to I flat rib cage which would compress in a tight place.

F to G straight, powerful hindlegs, which are neither bow legged (hocks turned out), or cow hocked (hocks turned in). Good muscle development which is not bulging.

J back pads of feet are barely touching the ground, because the dog stands well up on his toes.

1985 Breed Standard

Characteristics—The terrier must present a lively, active and alert appearance. He should impress one with his fearless and happy disposition. It should be remembered that the Jack Russell is a working terrier and should retain these instincts. Nervousness, cowardice or over aggression should be discouraged. He should always appear confident.

General Appearance—A sturdy, tough terrier, very much on its toes all the time, measuring between 10″ and 15″ at the withers. The body length must be in proportion to the height and it should present a compact, balanced image. He should be in solid, hard condition.

Head—Should be well-balanced and in proportion to the body. The skull should be flat, of moderate width at the ears, narrowing to the eyes. There should be a defined stop but not over-pronounced. The length of the muzzle from the nose to the stop should be slightly shorter than the distance from the stop to the occiput. The nose should be black. The jaw should be powerful, well-boned, with strongly muscled cheeks.

Eyes—Should be almond-shaped, dark in color and full of life and intelligence.

Ears—Small "V"-shaped drop ears carried forward close to the head and of moderate thickness.

Mouth—Strong teeth with the top teeth slightly overlapping the lower teeth (called a scissor bite).

Neck—Clean and muscular, of good length, gradually widening at the shoulders.

Forequarters—The shoulders should be sloping and well laid back, fine at points and clearly cut at the withers. Forelegs should be strong and straight boned with joints in correct alignment. Elbows hanging perpendicular to the body and working free of the sides.

Body—The chest should be shallow, narrow and the front legs set not too widely apart, giving an athletic, rather than heavily chested appearance. As a guide only, the chest should be small enough to easily be spanned behind the shoulders, by average size man's hands, when the terrier is in a fit, working condition. The back should be strong, straight and, in comparison to the height of the terrier, give a balanced image. The loin should be slightly arched.

Hindquarters—Should be strong and muscular, well put together with good angulation and bend of stifle, giving plenty of drive and propulsion. Looking from behind, the hocks must be straight.

Feet—Round, hard padded, of cat like appearance, neither turning in nor out.

Tail—Should be set rather high, carried gaily and in proportion to body length, usually about 4" long, providing a good hand-hold.

Coat—Smooth, without being so sparse as not to provide a certain amount of protection from the elements and undergrowth. Rough or broken coated, without being wooly.

Color—White should predominate with tan, black or brown markings. Brindle markings are not allowed.

Gait—Movement should be free, lively, well-coordinated with straight action in front and behind.

Please Note—For showing purposes, terriers are classified in two groups: 10" to 12½"; over 12½" up to 15".

Old scars or injuries, the result of work or accident, should not be allowed to prejudice a terrier's chance in the show ring unless they interfere with its movement or with its utility for work or stud.

Male animals should have two apparently normal testicles fully descended into the scrotum.

A Jack Russell Terrier should not show any strong characteristics of another breed.

Faults—Shyness. Disinterest. Overly aggressive. Defects in bite. Weak jaws. Fleshy ears. Pricked ears. Down at shoulder. Too much width between front legs. Barrel ribs. Out at elbow. Narrow hips. Straight stifle. Weak feet. Sluggish or unsound movement. Dishing. Plaiting. Toeing. Silky or woolly coats. Shrill or weak voice. Lack of muscle or skin tone. Lack of stamina or lung reserve. Evidence of foreign blood. Blue eye(s).

Examples of a rough coat. These two heads fill the requirement for a head as in the J.R.T.C.A. Breed Standard.

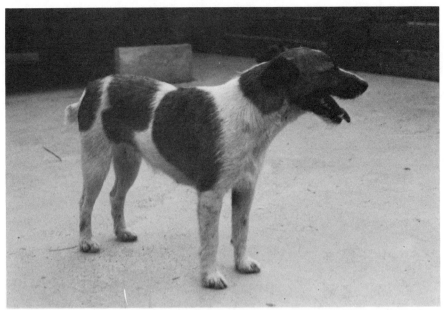

CRINKLE. Imported by Carol and Donald Philhower, from the Teem Valley Hunt, Wales. He is huntsman to the Golden's Bridge Hunt, North Salem, N.Y. This bitch is an excellent type. Her front and back legs are perfectly straight, as viewed from the front and back. Both the bottom and top line of the body are correct. She has a lovely head and neck, the latter flowing into a well sloped, flat shoulder. The width between the front legs is just right and there is enough depth behind the elbows to allow for plenty of lung room, but not so deep as to make squeezing into a small hole too difficult. She would be considered to have a broken coat. Notice the round foot, with the back pad barely touching the ground. CRINKLE was grand champion Jack Russell Terrier at the Terrier Annual Show in Connecticut 1984.

WOODLUCK GALLAHAD. A perfect ear set. Owned by José Rico, Conn.

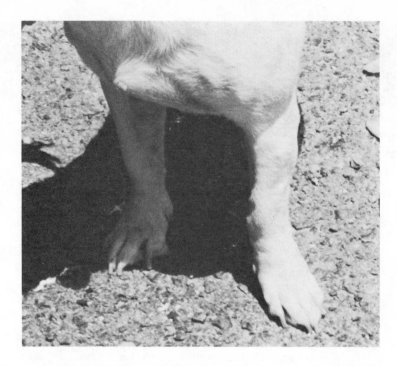

Incorrect: *Feet are weak and turn out badly. Toes are too long and not held tightly against each other. The foot is so flat that the dog has a lot of weight on his back pad.*

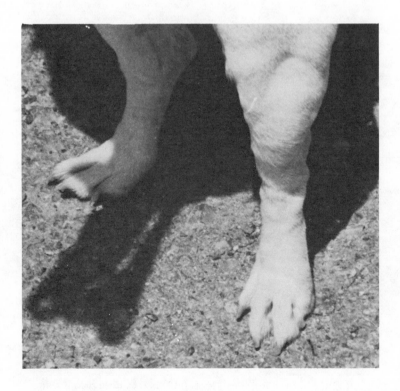

Even young puppies must have straight-legs, as this ten week old puppy shows. Note length of neck, good shoulder attachment and "not-too-wide" a chest.

*Hock (e.g. hind leg) does not go past vertical when terrier is trotting and has his **full weight** on the foot.*

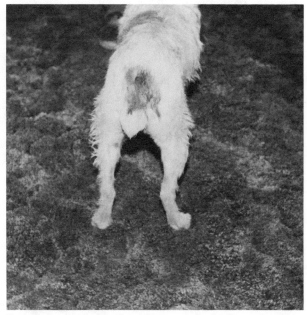

Correct: *hips, hocks, lower leg and feet are in a straight, perpendicular line.*

Incorrect: *hocks bend inside perpendicular line, toes point out.*

TEMPEST, the author's first Jack Russell Terrier bred and chosen for her by Bert Pateman, kennel huntsman to the Duke of Beaufort, England, owned by her daughter Caroline Treviranus.

*Here TEMPEST is showing correct and elegant movement. Notice how the hind leg is working **ahead** of the perpendicular.*

Courtesy Middletown Pony Club

Why a Breed Standard?

In 1975, when the Jack Russell Club of Great Britain was founded, it drew up a breed standard for the Jack Russell Terrier. This breed standard was adopted by the Jack Russell Terrier Club of America when it was founded the following year. The name, Jack Russell Terrier was adopted in order to give these white hunt terriers a name that would not arouse the anti-blood sport groups in Great Britain, who would appear in numbers any time there was anything to do with "HUNT." So, in order to avoid these groups at Hunt Terrier Trials, the word "hunt" was left out and they became Jack Russell Trials. The standard was drawn up in an effort to make these terriers uniform and to develop a breed that would be as close as possible to the terriers used by the Parson Jack Russell— hence the name. The following is an attempt to explain the requirements in the standard.

Under General Appearance the height, between ten and fifteen inches, is determined by concluding how short or tall a terrier could be, and still do his work underground in very small and often difficult places. The body and legs as measured from the top of the shoulder (withers) to the ground must be the same length as the back as measured from the withers to the base of the tail, in order to produce a dog that is well balanced, with a back that is short enough to be strong over the loins. It should not be so short, however, that the terrier is inflexible and therefore has trouble wriggling underground and handling any sharp turns. A back can be so short, as is the case with a cutting Quarter Horse, that jogging and galloping cannot be a completely relaxed ground-eating gait. A terrier with a long back tires quickly, does not have a lot of strength in the "rear-end" and will have difficulty maintaining any weight while in hard work. Legs that are too short are unsuitable for covering any distance, as when running with foxhounds. They are *not* stronger than a longer leg; and because they cannot reach beyond his muzzle, are unable to protect his face while underground. Long legs do not impede a terrier going to ground, as he goes to ground on his side (when the hole is small) and the length of leg makes no difference. A dog that would spread his front legs, spider like, when put into a hole and thus make it difficult for him to enter because his legs push against the sides, is not a sport as he obviously either doesn't know his work, or doesn't want any part of it.

The requirement for the head is merely a description of an intelligent, working head, one with plenty of brain-room, but which remains sharp and handsome in appearance. Too long a muzzle produces weakness in the jaw and too short, not enough jaw room. The nose must be black because it shows a lack of pigment when it is otherwise.

The ears are small, so as not to get caught in briars, or bitten by the adversary. Also, big ears suggest foreign blood. They must be close to the head and act as "ear-muffs," keeping out rain, snow, wind, etc., and falling dirt when underground.

The length of neck is one of the less important points. Basically, the terrier needs a strong neck, for protection and for worrying his quarry. Too short a neck, however, will surely finish up in a loaded shoulder and a wide chest. On the other hand there is nothing more pleasing to the eye than a head that is well set onto the neck (with a slight arch at the throat) which runs gracefully into a well laid back shoulder (meaning a shoulder with a good slope to it). The withers should not be thick (fatty). When standing over the terrier, the shoulders will look flat. They should be narrow at the top and then flare out to where the forelegs are attached. When this is the case, the rib cage will also be flat and will have spring to it, meaning it can be somewhat compressed, which a round ribcage cannot. Viewed from the front, the forelegs should not be too far apart. All this "front-end" conformation allows the terrier to flop on his side and squirm into tight places where a fox, who is a small animal, might have gone when hard pressed by hounds. The forelegs are straight because, inspite of what many people believe, a crooked, misshapen leg, is *NOT* stronger for digging, any more than a man with crooked arms is a superior weight lifter; or a horse with crooked front legs is a sounder race horse. The terrier's legs must work freely from his sides so that jogging and running appears effortless and ground devouring. Particularly serious are legs that are set on so that the elbows poke into the ribs, completely restricting his movement. Elbows that turn out aren't much better!

KATE—An excellent example of a terrier using her hocks forward and under her, not all strung out behind. Owned by Victor Heerman, Kentucky.

The rib cage, right behind the shoulders (the girth) should have some depth to it. If the girth is too shallow, the lungs will be small, as this is where they lie. Conversely, if the girth is too deep, the terrier will have difficulty going to ground. It is to be remembered that lungs are FLAT, so the width of the chest has nothing to do with lung room. It is the depth that gives the room. For that reason the speed dogs all have an exaggerated depth through the chest but are very narrow when viewed from the front. When the chest is spanned at the girth by a man's hands, using his third fingers and thumbs, they should meet.

The body, as mentioned above, should not be long, the line across the top should be straight, but may have a slight arch over the loin which gives him a longer reach with his hind legs when galloping and more power in his back. Under no circumstances should it have any sign of a hollow—this is a definite weakness. The bottom line should not be straight, but have a small arch from the girth back to waist. If the male terrier's sheath is small and tight it is a sign of strength; a big fatty sheath is unattractive and is associated with a non-athletic dog.

The hindquarters are the "tractor" part of the terrier. Without great strength in this area his digging ability and work underground is greatly lessened. It requires rear end power to dig underground, to fight underground and most important, to BACK out from underground, which is the way a terrier comes out of a small hole. The hindquarters should have a long line from the croup to the base of the tail and from the point of the hip to the point of the buttock. The tail, which should be approximately 4 inches long, should be set fairly high and carried gaily at approximately a 20° to 40° angle to the perpendicular, but should not have a large curl or be carried past the perpendicular over the back. The hind legs as seen from the side, should have some angulation, but not an exaggerated amount. This will put his hocks so they come behind the vertical; more than likely he will trot like a deer, with too much action, which is tiring and unattractive. The hock should work forward and stay under him when he trots. The gaskin muscle as seen from the side should be flat, long and wide. A bulging, narrow muscle is not as strong. When you look at the terrier from behind there should be good width between the hips, the legs should be neither bowlegged or cowhocked (hocks bending into each other, like a cow). The terrier should not only have straight legs when looked at from both front and back, but the action must be absolutely straight, in order to have an efficient, strong mover.

The feet should be fairly round, not long like a rabbit's foot. The toes should be slightly arched and have large strong nails that are kept trimmed so they don't break off during digging. These are feet that will not break down if the terrier does a lot of travelling and will have the strength to dig in difficult places.

The coat has to be coarse (versus fine) no matter what length it is, in order to give protection to the terrier. A rough coated dog should not give a wild and wooly impression. All hair should be straight, not wavy or curly. The coat, undercoat and skin should have an oily, not dry, feel in order to shed water, mud, etc. easily and quickly.

The Jack Russell Terrier is at least fifty percent white so that when he comes from an earth, not only covered with dirt, but smelling like a fox because they have been underground together, the waiting hounds will not mistake him for a fox. They have been known to do this with terriers who were mostly brown, with fatal results.

Basically the standard is drawn to produce a good-moving, efficient working dog that is a pleasure to look at and who is physically able to perform his job in the easiest, least tiring way. If he gives the appearance of self-assurance, cheerfulness, alertness and has an air about him that says he can hardly wait to get on with the job, you can be sure he is a terrier who is fit to do what he was bred to do—go-to-ground, stand up to his quarry and make such a racket that the handler above knows where to dig. These special traits make him a great sport in any situation involving hunting, play and comradeship as the many stories in this book have told.

So a Jack Russell Terrier, who comes from generations that have been bred to conform to the breed standard and to work well up to their quarry; and who have been selected for breeding because of their personality, intelligence and courage befitting a Jack Russell, is indeed a very special dog, ABOVE AND BELOW GROUND.